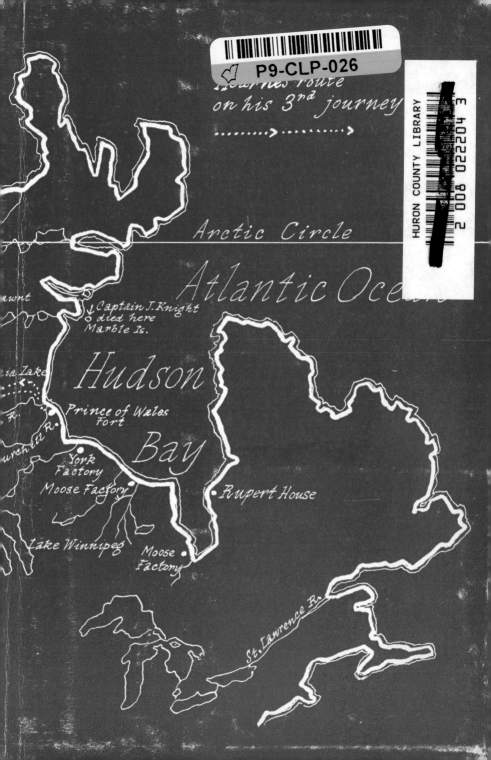

Hearnes route
on his 3rd journey

Arctic Circle

Atlantic Ocean

↓ Captain J. Knight
○ died here
Marble Is.

...ia Lake

Hudson

...R.

Prince of Wales
Fort

...urchill R.

Bay

York
Factory

Moose Factory

· Rupert House

Lake Winnipeg

Moose
Factory

St. Lawrence R.

...awnt

ON FOOT TO
THE ARCTIC

The Story of Samuel Hearne

By Ronald Syme

Illustrated by WILLIAM STOBBS

WILLIAM MORROW & COMPANY
New York 1959

Third Printing, May 1967

Library of Congress Catalog Card No. 59-5530

CONTENTS

ON FOOT TO THE ARCTIC

Chapter One

Sailor and Fur Trader

THE English county of Somerset was a good place for any boy to live. The streams which flowed through the fine green meadows were filled with small trout and perch. In forest glades of oak and elm and ash, big cock pheasants made an easy target for anyone expert with a sling and able to dodge the prowling wardens. In the kitchens of the white-walled farmhouses, great joints of beef frizzled gently in copper pans, and the warm air was filled with the aroma of smoked ham, cheese, fresh butter, and sweet West Country honey.

Young Samuel Hearne was born in Somerset in the year 1745. His father, a local grain merchant, died a few years later. The grain business was sold after his death, and Samuel, together with his mother, went to live in a small cottage on a very small income.

The shortage of money at home never worried Samuel. By holding horses for the gentlemen who came to the village tavern, he could always earn a penny or two with which to buy a couple of fishhooks or a length of wire for a rabbit snare. At the age of nine he was a sturdy youngster in patched homespun clothes who was already learning the ways of a poacher.

The only problem Samuel had was that during his school hours he could never forget the interesting things he had seen in the woods or fields the day before. He was a clever artist, and sometimes he tried drawing fish or birds or animals when he should have been working. Somehow or other, the schoolmaster nearly always found out.

"What are you doing, Hearne?"

"Nothing, sir."

"Indeed! Pray, give me that piece of paper you are hiding."

"It's . . . it's only a picture, sir."

"So I see. Why are you drawing squirrels, Hearne, when the others are studying Latin?"

"I . . . I don't know, sir."

"You don't know? Pray, have the goodness to step out here and hand me yonder birch."

For a few days after his latest whipping, Samuel Hearne would try to think only of his work in school. But his mind was too full of interesting memories of the countryside. Sooner or later, the master would catch him again with an unfinished picture of a pike snatching eagerly at a frog in a deep pool, or a partridge scurrying hastily through the grass.

When Samuel was eleven years old, the village schoolmaster went to see Mrs. Hearne. "Ma'am," he said, "it grieves me to cause you trouble, but I must—I really must—ask you to withdraw Samuel from my school. He is learning nothing, and his idleness is setting a bad example for his companions."

Mrs. Hearne sighed. "Yes, I know. He is a good boy at home, but he seems to think of little except wandering about the countryside. Pray, sir, how would you advise me to try to improve his ways?"

"Send the young gentleman to sea, ma'am," said the angry schoolmaster. "I warrant you they'll discipline him in the Navy."

Oddly enough, Samuel liked the idea of going to sea. None of his ancestors had been sailors, and it is doubtful that he had ever seen the ocean. But there was seafaring blood in the veins of the men of Somerset, and for centuries past many of them had been sailors. Even so, Hearne might not have been quite so ready to join the Navy if he had known what kind of a life it meant for him.

The laws of England in those days were terribly severe. A court once sentenced an eight-year-old boy to death for stealing a pot of paint valued at twopence. Another court ordered an eleven-year-old girl to be deported for life for dressing up in boy's clothes and borrowing a farmer's horse. But naval laws were even harsher than those ashore. Out of a list of thirty-six crimes which seamen might commit, twenty-two were punishable by death if the captain of the ship ordered it. For stealing even a small piece of tobacco, a sailor was punished by having boiling pitch poured over his head. Afterward he was put ashore and left on the first land the vessel sighted, even if it was a wild African beach, or an icebound island.

Living conditions on board ship were equally severe. The sleeping quarters were damp and crowded, and the only kinds of food for officers and men were salt beef, salt pork, dried pea soup, and rocklike biscuits which were filled with horrid yellow weevils. There were no fresh vegetables or fruit of any kind, and on a long voyage it was quite usual for at least half the crew to die of scurvy, an illness caused by lack of fresh foods. The drinking water after six weeks at sea was yellow, stinking, and alive with germs. And for working under these horrible conditions, the English seaman was paid twenty-five shillings ($3.50) per month.

Samuel Hearne was eleven years old when he agreed to join the Navy. It was lucky for him that Captain Hood, a naval officer who was to become an admiral in later years, had a country estate in Somerset. The Captain knew Samuel by sight, and perhaps he suspected that this tall youngster with the quick blue eyes and pleasant face might have lifted a pheasant or two from his own estate. But Captain Hood was a bit of a buccaneer himself, and he could admire that same spirit in others. That may have been the reason why he wrote a letter concerning Samuel to the Admiralty. As a result of that letter, Samuel became a midshipman instead of an ordinary seaman.

Conditions on board ship were only slightly better for midshipmen than for sailors. They, too, were wretchedly crowded together, miserably paid, and taught their duties with a leather strap or length of rope. Any boy who could endure such conditions would never fear hardship or danger again. Those who couldn't, either left the Navy as soon as possible, or died at sea of scurvy or fever. Samuel was one of those who survived the hardships of the life.

"I found the lessons in navigation most interesting," he wrote, "and my knowledge of seamanship improved quickly with every voyage. Being of robust health, I remained free of sickness, even when the greater part of the ship's company was suffering from one disorder or another."

Hearne did not choose to mention the fact that he fought in many sea battles against the French, and that he sent his entire share of prize money to his widowed mother in Somerset.

Promotion in the Navy was very slow. Unless an officer was the son of a wealthy family or had powerful friends to help him, he was not likely to rise to the command of a vessel. Hearne, being a somewhat impatient young man who preferred to make his own way, grew tired of waiting. He had an idea there were better chances for him elsewhere. For instance, the Hudson's Bay Company had been growing in wealth and power in Canada for nearly a hundred years. The Company was running trading vessels of its own up in the cold salt waters of of the Bay. Surely there would be a vacancy for a young naval officer on one of those ships.

Samuel went to London and paid a visit to the directors of the Hudson's Bay Company. The directors liked the look of this burly young officer with the blue eyes and yellow hair. They could see that Hearne was strong and healthy, and they knew that any man who could endure life in the Navy for nine years was thoroughly accustomed to hardship and danger.

"As it happens, Mr. Hearne," they said, "there is a vacancy as mate aboard the Company's whaling sloop, the *Churchill,* now operating in Hudson Bay. We are prepared to appoint you to the position. Your wages will be fifty pounds ($150) a year, and you may receive a small share of the profits. Do you agree to this?"

The salary was higher than Hearne's pay as a senior midshipman. Besides, he felt sure that he would find life aboard a whaler less monotonous than naval life. "Indeed yes, gentlemen," he replied. "I will be ready to join the *Churchill* as soon as I get my discharge from the Navy."

Hearne reached Hudson Bay in the year 1765, when he was twenty years old.

"At that time," he wrote, "my knowledge of Canada was very slight, and my diligent search for written works describing this vast country had not yet met with much success. Most of the books I consulted were in French, a language with which I was very unfamiliar."

No wonder that Samuel Hearne could find so little information about Canada. Until 1759, only six years earlier, Canada had belonged to France. Wars between England and France were so frequent in those days that any Englishman who entered Canada was likely to find himself in prison at Quebec or Montreal or Three Rivers the moment a new war began. The French, jealous of their prosperous fur trade, were naturally unwilling to allow the English, whom they detested, to collect much information about Canada.

Only in Hudson Bay, far to the north, had English traders managed to set themselves up in the country. Ever since 1670, the Hudson's Bay Company had been building fortified trading posts round the southern end of the Bay. These wooden-walled forts were attacked by the French by land and sea. French and English warships fought one another in Hudson Bay. Raiding parties of daring young Frenchmen, traveling by canoe and snowshoes, came northward from Montreal to attack the Company's forts.

Bales of furs were destroyed, forts were

burned, and men were killed; but in spite of all
this the English managed to remain in Hudson
Bay. Rich profits could be made from the fur
trade, and it was worth the Company's while to
spend a great deal of money building forts, buy-
ing heavy guns, and arming the trading vessels
which carried the precious cargoes of furs out of
the Bay and to London. There was never a time
when the French were able to seize all the
Hudson's Bay Company's forts at once, and
those that were not captured shipped enough
furs to England to enable the Company to go on
making a profit.

These were dangerous years for Englishmen
in this region, and few of them cared to go far
beyond the walls of their forts. All around lay
hundreds of miles of barren country, or dark
forests where a man might lose his way and die
of cold or hunger. There were icy rivers and
swamps and unknown tribes of Indians whose
warriors might kill a wandering white man for
the sake of his scalp, his musket, and the contents
of his pack. Every year the directors of the
Hudson's Bay Company wrote vainly to the gov-
ernors of their forts:

"Choose out from amongst our Servants such as are best qualified with Strength of Body and the Indian Language to travel and to discover the country. For their encouragement we shall plentifully reward them."

During the first period of the Company's history in the Bay, only one man had been brave enough to volunteer for exploration. He was twenty-year-old Henry Kelsey, who had traveled as far westward as Manitoba in 1690. But when Samuel Hearne reached Canada in 1765, the Company was gloomily realizing that it had not kept its hundred-year-old promise to the British government to explore the country. The coast of Hudson Bay had been explored, and that was about all. Hearne wrote in his diary that his knowledge of Canada was "very slight," but no one else knew more than he about the country which lay to the west and north of the Company's forts. The French had gone, but the forests, the cruel winters, and the Indian tribes remained.

The *Churchill* was a heavy-timbered little ship, manned by freely spoken English and Scots seamen. It was loaded with harpoon tackle and reeked with a stink of whale oil. Samuel Hearne found life aboard the whaler very different from naval life. Neither the wandering parties of Indians on the shore nor the Eskimos in their sealskin-tent settlements could be trusted very far. There were unknown rocks and shoals, and treacherous gales and fogs were always awaiting a chance to send a small vessel to destruction on the lonely coast.

> "The walrus often attack small boats merely from spite," Hearne wrote in his diary. "They not only put the crew in great confusion but also in great danger, for they always aim at staving in the boat with their tusks, or try to get into the boat."

One day, a few months after Hearne's arrival in Hudson Bay, his crew were rowing him across to an islet when a large number of walrus appeared out of the coldly glittering sea and surrounded the boat. Hearne was always interested in any new kind of animal or bird or fish, but on this occasion he had little time to study these walrus, which quickly began to attack the boat.

> "Notwithstanding the crew's utmost attempts to keep them off, one walrus, more daring than the

rest, though a small one, got in over the stern, and after sitting and looking at the people some time, he again plunged into the water to his companions. At that instant another, of an enormous size, was getting in over the bow; and every other means proving useless to prevent such an unwelcome visit, the bowman took up a gun loaded with goose shot, put the muzzle into the creature's mouth, and shot him dead. The walrus immediately sank and was followed by all his companions. The crew then made their way to the vessel and arrived just before the walrus were ready to make their second attack. This might have been worse than the first, as the creatures seemed much enraged at the loss of their companion."

Hudson Bay was a bleak and lonely place. The eastern coast was treeless and rocky, with little shelter for ships for hundreds of miles. In James Bay, at the southern end of Hudson Bay, dark-green forests stood along a low shore line. Flowers and grass appeared during the few short months of summer, only to vanish when icy winter approached. Along the west coast grew more forests. Behind them lay treacherous areas of frozen muskeg, or tracts of bog. In the winter, when the Bay was covered with ice, the crew of the *Churchill* lived ashore in thick-walled huts, where water froze at a distance of fifteen feet from roaring iron stoves.

Hearne's years of seafaring life had not cured him of his love of wandering. Often when he stood on the *Churchill's* deck, he gazed toward the distant horizon of dark forest or barren plain. It was lonely, hostile, and empty country, utterly unknown to any European. But it was vast and new to Hearne, and he envied the wild duck, the swan, and the eagles for the ease with which they could soar over territory in their migratory flights which a man could cross only on foot.

Hearne knew nothing of the hardships of travel in the far North: the everlasting search for food, the trackless wastes where a man once lost might wander forever, and the killing cold of blizzards. He only knew the friendly woods and meadows of Somerset and the little world of a ship at sea. In spite of his ignorance, or perhaps because of it, he grew eager to explore this empty wilderness of river and hill and plain.

He might not have become an explorer if the Company had not promoted him to a larger ship. Hearne was a quick-tempered and outspoken young man who disliked slackness or foolishness of any kind. He had learned his seamanship in the British Navy, and his ideas about how a ship should be run were certainly different from those of the easygoing masters in charge of the Company's vessels. At any rate, he seems to have had an argument, or perhaps several arguments, with his new captain. He wrote:

> "Mr. Joseph Stephens, in the year 1767, had the command of the *Charlotte* given him, a fine brig of one hundred tons, when I was his Mate. He was a man of the least merit I ever knew."

This was merely another way of saying that he regarded Mr. Joseph Stephens as an incompetent ass. And whenever an officer begins to feel like that about his captain, it is time for him to look for another ship.

Hearne took another step instead. He wrote to the Company in London and asked to be given employment in one of the trading posts ashore. Back came a letter appointing him to the staff at Prince of Wales Fort on the west coast of Hudson Bay. The directors must have liked young Hearne; otherwise he would not have been given a job for which he had no training.

But before Hearne left the *Charlotte,* he saw something which warned him of the dangers of exploration in northern Canada. It was the remains of an old tragedy.

In the year 1719, the Company had become interested in Indian stories of rich copper mines somewhere beyond the northwestern end of Hudson Bay. All Europe at that time was still wondering whether a Northwest Passage for ships could be found somewhere up in the arctic. Such a passage would allow ships to pass swiftly from the Atlantic to the Pacific and so to the rich trade of the East Indies. The Company decided to send two ships to the northern end of Hudson Bay to search for copper and also for a sea passage running from east to west.

James Knight, an old veteran trader with seafaring experience, was placed in command of an expedition of two ships, the *Albany* and the *Discovery.* The vessels sailed for Hudson Bay in the summer of 1719, and they were not heard of again for forty-eight years.

At last the *Charlotte,* with Samuel Hearne as mate, came to anchor at bleak and little-known Marble Island at the northwestern end of Hud-

son Bay. There they found traces of those missing men who had met death in the arctic.

"The boats discovered a new harbor at the East
end of Marble Island, at the head of which they
found guns, anchors, cables, bricks, a smith's anvil,
and many other articles which the hand of time had
not defaced. The remains of a house, though pulled
to pieces by the Eskimos for the wood and iron, are
yet very plain to be seen, as are also the hulls of two
ships which lie sunk in about five fathoms [thirty
feet] of water towards the head of the harbor. The
figurehead of one ship, and also the guns, were sent
home to the Company, and are certain proofs that
Mr. Knight had been lost on that inhospitable island,
where neither stick nor stump is to be seen, and
which lies sixteen miles from the mainland. This
mainland is little better, being a jumble of barren
hills and rocks, without any kind of herbage except
moss and grass, and at that part the woods are
several hundreds of miles from the seashore."

Through an Eskimo interpreter, Samuel
Hearne discovered what had happened to the
men on the ships.

"When the vessels arrived at Marble Island, it was
very late in the autumn, and in getting into the
harbor the larger vessel received much damage.

Then the Englishmen began to build their house, their number at that time seeming to be about fifty. As soon as the ice permitted in the following Summer (one thousand seven hundred and twenty), the Eskimos paid another visit, by which time the number of Englishmen was greatly reduced. . . . In 1721 they only found five of the Englishmen alive, and those were in such distress for food that they eagerly ate seal's flesh and whale's blubber quite raw. This made them so sick that three of them died in a few days. The other two, though very weak, managed to bury them. Those two survived many days after the rest, and frequently went to the top of a nearby rock and earnestly looked to the South and East as if expecting some vessels to come to their relief. After continuing there for a considerable time together, and nothing appearing in sight, they sat down close together and wept bitterly. At length one of the two died, and the other's strength was so exhausted that he fell down and died also, in attempting to dig a grave for his companion."

Hearne was a courageous young man. Otherwise, the sad relics he had seen at Marble Island and the sad story told him by the Eskimos might have discouraged forever his ambition to become an explorer. Even to this day, Eskimos landing on Marble Island drop to their knees and creep across the narrow beach out of respect for the memory of James Knight, shipwright and master mariner, and the Englishmen who died with him more than two hundred years ago.

Chapter Two

The Fort Beside the Sea

GRANITE-WALLED Prince of Wales Fort stood on the west coast of Hudson Bay beside the mouth of the Churchill River. Its buildings were enclosed within a square formed by lofty walls one hundred yards in length. It had taken over thirty years to complete, and English masons had cut every one of the great blocks of stone by hand. Laboring gangs had hauled these

stones on clumsy sledges to the site of the growing fort.

The Company had grown tired of having their log forts battered down by French cannon fire and their precious cargoes of furs seized by the invaders. They were determined that Prince of Wales Fort should be able to hold off any attacks. Guns of heavy caliber were mounted on the walls, and the surrounding countryside was cleared of straggly bushes, grass, and rocks for a distance of one mile, so that attackers would have no shelter from gunfire as they advanced on the fort.

Inside the fort lived the employees of the Company. They were a queer crowd of men. Some of them had come to Canada to escape trouble at home; many were Scotsmen from the Orkney Islands, whom a Company official described as "close, prudent, quiet people, strictly faithful to their employers and unpleasantly mean."

To Prince of Wales Fort, as well as the other five trading posts belonging to the Company at that time, came parties of Indians with furs to barter for European goods. The prices they

were to receive were strictly fixed in the Company's list of regulations. A brass kettle cost one beaver skin. A short musket cost twelve beaver; one gallon of English brandy, four beaver; two hatchets, one beaver; one and a half pounds of gunpowder, one beaver; one blanket, six beaver; and so on. The trouble was that these trading parties of Indians always demanded enormous quantities of presents in addition to what they were paid for the pelts they brought. The tribes living round Hudson Bay were a worse type than those which dwelt on the plains of the West: the Sioux, the Blackfeet, and others. Hearne never really grew to like them, and one can easily understand why.

"If a Governor of a fort denies them anything they ask," he wrote, "though it be only to give away to the most useless of their gang, they immediately turn sulky and impertinent to the highest degree. However sensible they may be at other times, they become utterly stupid on these occasions and raise their demands to so high a pitch that after they have received to the amount of five times the value of all the furs they have brought, they never cease begging during their stay at the Factory [fort] and, after all, few of them go away thoroughly satisfied."

Yet there were many things about his life at Prince of Wales Fort which Hearne enjoyed. His stone-walled house at the fort was much larger than his little cabin aboard the *Charlotte*, and blazing log fires kept it reasonably warm even on the coldest nights. He had plenty of chances to study the habits of wild animals and birds, and he was becoming a good amateur naturalist. He built a pond for beaver in which they lived during the summer months, and he was able to make a careful study of their habits.

"When the weather became very cold," he wrote, "I was obliged to take them into my house. I gave them a large tub of water, and they made not the least dirt, though they were kept in my own sitting room. They became the constant companions of the Indian men and women and were so fond of their company that when the Indians were absent for any length of time, the beaver showed great signs of uneasiness. On the people's return, the creatures showed equal pleasure by crawling into their laps, lying on their backs, sitting erect like squirrels, and behaving to them like children who see their parents but seldom. In general, during the winter they lived on the same food as the women did, and were remarkably fond of rice and plum pudding."

Also encamped in Hearne's living quarters were various other pets, which were much more interesting than the moles, rabbits, hedgehogs, and mice he had kept as a boy. Of his tame ermine he wrote:

"In winter it was of a delicate white all over, except the tip of its tail, which was of a glossy black. I took much trouble to tame this beautiful animal but could never succeed, for the longer I kept it, the more restless and impatient it became."

Muskrats, he wrote, "are easily tamed and soon grow fond [affectionate], are very cleanly and playful, and smell exceedingly pleasant of musk." A squirrel Hearne kept was "so familiar as to take anything out of my hand, and sit on the table where I was writing and play with the pens. Yet it could never bear to be handled, was very mischievous, gnawing the chair bottoms, window curtains, sashes, etc., to pieces." Hearne was less fortunate in his attempt to make friends with a small otter. "In a very short time they are so fond that it is scarcely possible to keep them from climbing up one's legs and body, and they never feel happier than when sitting

on the shoulder. But when angry or frightened, they emit a very disagreeable smell, like the skunk, which renders them quite disgusting."

The other men in the fort regarded Hearne as a peculiar sort of fellow, for none of them took the least interest in Canada, Indians, or wildlife. Indeed, most of them detested the barren countryside, and while the Orkney Islanders spent much of their spare time counting their money, the Englishmen spent theirs grumbling or catching bad colds in the head.

"Always messing around with queer creatures," they said of Hearne. "When he hasn't got a hairy-tailed mouse tucked away inside his shirt, he's drawing pictures of a beaver splashing about in a bathtub, or fiddling away with a compass and maps of heaven knows where."

During Hearne's first winter at Prince of Wales Fort, two scientists, William Wales and Joseph Dymond, came from England to make astronomical observations of the planet Venus. They were a pleasant pair of men, and they soon made friends with Hearne, the only other person in the fort who knew anything about stars and latitudes and longitudes. The Company's staff

did not begin working until eight in the morning
in winter, and because of the early darkness,
work ended with the tolling of a bell at four
o'clock. Hearne was left with plenty of time on
his hands. He spent it reading the scientific
books which Wales and Dymond had brought
from England, and asking them questions as
they sat close beside a blazing fire during the
long and bitter evenings. The two scientists
went back to England, but they left Hearne with
a lot of new ideas and a greatly improved educa-
tion in scientific matters.

The governor of Prince of Wales Fort was a
half-caste Indian named Moses Norton. It seems
strange that the respectable Company should
have given him such a responsible position, for
to put it mildly, Norton was a very queer person
indeed. He had spent about nine years in England and had learned to speak excellent English.
On his return to Canada, however, he went back
to the unpleasant way of life led by his Indian
countrymen. Hearne loathed Norton, and so did
the other Europeans in the fort. One of Norton's
habits was to stand over the men engaged in
enlarging the fort and strike them with a whip

when the work went too slowly. But he had
other unpleasant habits as well. This is what
Samuel Hearne had to say about him:

> "He married five or six of the finest Indian girls
> he could select, but took every means in his power
> to prevent any European from having anything to
> do with the women of the country. To his own
> friends and their country he was so attached that he
> showed more respect to one of their favorite dogs
> than he ever did to his first officer. Amongst his
> miserable and ignorant countrymen he passed as a
> doctor, and always kept a box of poison to give to
> those who refused to allow him to marry their
> daughters.
>
> "His apartments were not only convenient but
> elegant, and always crowded with favorite Indians.
> As he advanced in years, his jealousy increased. He
> actually poisoned two of his wives, because he
> thought they preferred younger men. He was a
> most notorious smuggler, but though he put many
> thousands into the pockets of the Captains [tribal
> chiefs], he seldom put a shilling into his own.
>
> "This I declare to be the real character and man-
> ner of life of the late Mr. Moses Norton."

In spite of beating his workmen with a whip,
marrying any number of wives, and poisoning
his fellow countrymen, Mr. Norton was inclined

to be reasonably honest with the Company's money! It would have been easy for Hearne not to have mentioned this one good quality the half-caste Governor possessed, but being fair-minded, he did include it in his description.

The English king, Charles II, had given the the Hudson's Bay Company the whole trade "of all those seas, straits, and bays, rivers, lakes, creeks, and sounds" around Hudson Bay. But in return the Company had promised to send its men westward and northward to explore. That was in the year 1670. Seventy-eight years later, in 1748, jealous rival merchants in England were claiming that the Company "had not discovered, or sufficiently attempted to discover, the North-west Passage into the southern seas [the Pacific Ocean]." The English Government began to ask questions, and the Company was reminded of its promise to send out explorers to map the unknown territories around Hudson Bay. The directors stated that they had done as much as they could to find the mysterious Northwest Passage. Indeed, they produced the following list of voyages of exploration in order to prove their words:

1719   *Albany Frigate*, Captain George Berley, sailed from England on or about June 5. Never returned.
Discovery, Captain David Vaughan, sailed from England June 5. Never returned.
Prosperous, Captain Henry Kelsey, sailed from York Fort June 19. Returned August 10.
Success, John Hancock, Master, sailed from Prince of Wales Fort July 2. Returned August 10.

1721   *Prosperous*, Captain Henry Kelsey, sailed from York Fort June 26. Returned September 2.
Whalebone, John Scroggs, Master, sailed from Gravesend [in London] May 31. Wintered at Prince of Wales Fort.

1722   *Whalebone*, sailed from Prince of Wales Fort. Returned July 25.

1737   *Churchill*, James Napper, Master, sailed from Prince of Wales Fort July 7. Died August 8, and the vessel returned the 18th.
Musquash, Robert Crow, Master, sailed from Prince of Wales Fort July 7. Returned August 22.

The English Government became satisfied that the Company had indeed searched properly for the Northwest Passage, but they suggested that men might have been sent to explore by land. The Company was as anxious as anyone else to find out about the territories to the north and west, but they pointed out that it was hard to find men willing to set off into an unknown wilderness. At the forts, or factories, as they were sometimes called, were coopers who made barrels for whale oil, armorers who mended guns free of charge for the Indians, masons and carpenters, and a number of clerks, servants, and junior assistants. How could explorers be found among such men?

Moses Norton had an idea that Samuel Hearne might be just the kind of man the Company needed. Hearne was working very hard at learning the Indian language and customs. He was a navigator and a good draftsman, and his life in the Navy and on the Hudson Bay whalers had accustomed him to hardships unknown to the ordinary landsman. Finally, Hearne had the courage and fine appearance—he was six feet in height and broad-shouldered—necessary for any European attempting to live in Indian camps among warriors of uncertain temper.

Norton was interested in the Indian rumor about copper mines somewhere up in the Arctic

Circle. He believed that there must be deposits of natural ore in that region, for Indians often appeared at the fort wearing ornaments of pure copper. Norton suggested to the Company in London that ships homeward bound from Hudson Bay could take cargoes of this ore instead of the useless rocks which they used as ballast. The vessels might even be able to anchor in the river where the copper was said to lie, an unknown river which had already been given the name of the Coppermine River.

Perhaps to Norton's surprise, twenty-four-year-old Hearne seemed quite pleased with the idea of risking his life in a cold and ugly wilderness. Governor Norton wrote a letter to the Company in London, and they, in turn, sent one to Hearne.

"Mr. Norton has proposed an inland Journey," they wrote, "far to the north of Churchill, to promote an extension of our trade, as well as for the discovery of a Northwest Passage, etc. An undertaking of this kind requires the attention of a person capable of making an observation for determining the longitude and latitude and also distances, and the course of rivers and their depths. Therefore we have fixed on you (especially as you are willing) to conduct this journey with proper assistants."

Having thus prepared to send Hearne on a journey during which he would be in constant danger of death by hunger, cold, or treacherous Indians, the directors ended their letter with the words: "We heartily wish you health and success in this present expedition, and remain your loving Friends."

Chapter Three

The Tenderfoot Explorer

HEARNE was one of the most inexperienced Europeans who ever set off to explore part of North America. Men such as La Salle, who mapped the Mississippi; Champlain, who discovered the Great Lakes; and Pierre Radisson, who found the overland route to Hudson Bay from Quebec, had spent years among the Indians and knew how to handle them. They were familiar with tribal customs and were trained backwoodsmen and hunters.

Poor Hearne had never spent a day in the wilds of northern Canada. The only Indians he had met were those who came to the fort to sell furs. He had never had to rely on his musket for food, and he had no idea where to look for game. He had never traveled on snowshoes, or by canoe, or lived in a tent. The only advantage he had over most explorers was his ability to use a compass and a quadrant, but on the other hand, he lacked the strange instinct that enabled some men to travel hundreds of miles through un-mapped country and return safely to their starting place.

The Company in London wrote another long letter to Hearne, setting out a list of all the tasks they hoped he would be able to accomplish. This is a typical paragraph from the letter:

"Your Indian guides will conduct you to a river said to abound with copper ore and animals of the fur kind. It is said to be so far to the northward that in the middle of summer the sun does not set, and is supposed by the Indians to empty itself into some ocean. This river is called by the northern Indians [the Chipewyan tribe] Neeth-fan-fan-dazey, or the Far-off Metal River. You are, if possible, to trace it to the mouth, and there determine the latitude and longitude as near as you can.

"Be careful to observe what mines are near the river, what water there is at the river's mouth, how far the woods are from the seaside, the course of the river, the nature of the soil. If the said river is likely to be of any use, take possession of it on behalf of the Hudson's Bay Company by cutting your name on some of the rocks, as also the date of the year, month, etc."

And so the letter continued. Comfortable, well-fed gentlemen in far-off London had written it. Many of them had never been in Canada; none of them knew anything about the hardships of exploration. They were thoughtful enough to add, however, that when Hearne came back from the Coppermine River with all the information they needed, they would give him a sum of money as a reward. They forgot, however, to supply him with any tools for cutting his name on the rocks.

Moses Norton unwisely chose two other Europeans to accompany Hearne. One was William

Ibester, an ex-sailor; the other was Thomas Merriman, a junior clerk. Neither of these men seemed very anxious to go exploring, and perhaps they did so only in order to escape the monotonous life and hard work at the fort.

On November 6, 1769, Norton gave Hearne a letter containing his orders and this statement: "Captain Chawchinahaw, his Lieutenant, Nabyah, and six or eight of the best northern [Chipewyan] Indians we can procure, with a small part of their families, are to conduct you, provide for you, and assist you and your companions." Two Indians of the Cree tribe were also chosen to go with Hearne. These men lived near the fort, spoke a little English, and were accustomed to European ways. Otherwise, they were about as useful as "Captain" Chawchinahaw and his precious "Lieutenant" Nabyah turned out to be.

Hearne's own preparations for the journey were very simple:

"I drew a Map on a large sheet of parchment and sketched all the West coast of the Bay on it, but left the interior parts blank, to be filled up during my journey. Ammunition, useful ironwork, some tobacco, a few knives, and other necessary articles make a sufficient load for anyone to carry when going on a journey likely to last twenty months or two years. As that was the case, I took only the shirt and clothes I then had on, one spare coat, a pair of breeches, and as much cloth as would make me two or three pair of Indian stockings. These, with a blanket for bedding, composed the whole of my stock of clothing."

Hearne and his companions left the fort on November 6, 1769. It was an odd time to set off on a journey anywhere, for the whole winter lay ahead of them. The Indians and their wives were wearing heavy suits of deerskin, but Hearne, who was able to endure cold as well as any Indian, still wore only his shirt, coat, and knee breeches. The ground was covered with early snow which had not yet frozen hard. The sledges, which the Indians hauled by deerskin bands passed round their chests and across their foreheads, kept breaking through the surface. Having to free them wasted time, and for the first couple of days, Hearne's party was able to cover only eight to ten miles between sunrise and sunset. One of the northern Indians then decided to take himself off during the night.

"As the rest of my crew were heavy-laden, I was under the necessity of hauling the sledge he had left, which, however, was not very heavy, as it scarcely exceeded sixty pounds."

Neither Ibester, the sailor, nor Merriman, the clerk, was able to help with the sledge. They were not as strong as Hearne, and they were already grumbling about the weight of their seventy-pound packs as they floundered on northward through the soft snow.

Bleak hills and small patches of wind-twisted pine trees stretched to the horizon. There was no cover for deer or other game, and Hearne became alarmed as he watched the supplies of food rapidly diminish. The Indians, however, went on eating as much as their stomachs could hold. Hearne had not yet discovered that these savages never worried about hunger tomorrow if they had enough to eat today. And Chawchinahaw, their leader, a gaunt, sour-faced fellow, preferred to tell a lie rather than cut down on his eating. "We will reach big woods in another four or five days," he said. "They will be filled with deer sheltering from the coming

winter. There will be plenty of venison for all of us."

That was on the ninth of November. Ten days later they had not yet reached the woods, and the covering of snow on the ground had become so thin that the sledges were breaking daily. Hearne and his two English companions were beginning to find out what hunger was like, and as the cold became greater, they came to know other hardships as well. There were nights in that bleak land when it was impossible to collect enough wood to make a fire. They made a place to sleep by digging a hole in the snow, lying down on the moss underneath, wrapping themselves in their clothing, and standing their sledges on edge to serve as a windbreak.

On November 21 they reached the woods Chawchinahaw had spoken of and found only a few gray hillsides, covered with miserable stunted pines and junipers. There was no sign of deer. A few partridge scuttled among the trees, and that was about all. The villainous Chawchinahaw had promised to see that his men kept Hearne supplied with food, but now they began to eat every partridge they shot. The three

Englishmen were very hungry indeed. The wretched Indians even failed to feed their own wives and children, and to save them from starvation, Hearne and the two Cree had to share with them the few birds they killed.

"Greater hunger awaits you ahead," Chawchinahaw declared sulkily to Hearne. "You and your two white friends will certainly die if you continue your journey. Let us give up this useless expedition and return to the fort."

"How do you know what lies ahead?" Hearne asked the Indian angrily. "You promised to lead us to the Far-off Metal River. Keep your promise now. Are you afraid of an empty belly and cold nights?"

"No," replied Chawchinahaw, in an offended and bad-tempered manner. "I am not afraid of such things. I want to go back to the fort, where my friend, the Governor, will give us all the food we want, so that we do not have to hunt for it daily."

"We are not going back," Hearne replied. "Not until we reach the Coppermine River."

Chawchinahaw realized that he had no chance of frightening his untrained, obstinate leader.

He tried another trick, which was more successful.

"He influenced several of the best northern Indians to desert in the night. They took with them several bags of my ammunition, some pieces of ironwork, such as hatchets, ice chisels, files, etc., as well as several other useful articles."

This was mutiny of the most treacherous kind. On a ship Hearne would have known how to deal with Chawchinahaw, but there was little he could do in this frozen wilderness of northern Canada. Probably Hearne was a little to blame himself. He was a very young man and had not yet learned how to control wild and lawless Indians. He was inclined to treat them too well, and the savages were repaying his kindness with treachery. Nor had Chawchinahaw, the Indian whom Moses Norton had chosen, yet finished his villainous work.

"Chawchinahaw added that he and the rest of his countrymen were going to strike off another way in order to join the remainder of their wives and families. He and his crew delivered me most of the things which they had in charge, and set out toward the Southwest, making the woods ring with their laughter. They left us to consider our unhappy situation: nearly two hundred miles from Prince of Wales Fort, all heavily laden, and our strength and spirits greatly reduced by hunger and fatigue."

Merriman, the clerk, was inclined to panic with fright, and Ibester, the sailor, was unhappy and silent. The end of November had arrived, and the icy blanket of winter was beginning to cover the whole countryside. The departing Indians had left no food behind them, and there was no sign of game. Death by cold and starvation seemed very close.

"We're going back to the fort," Hearne said. "We'll each carry a sixty-pound pack and haul a sledge as well. They'll run more easily over this frozen snow. Powder and shot are the first things we'll leave behind, for they weigh the most and cost the least."

Hearne took charge of his little party of two Englishmen and the two almost useless southern (Cree) Indians. With quadrant, chronometer, and compass he located his actual position and then set a course for the return journey southward to the fort.

"In the course of the day's walk we were fortunate enough to kill several partridge, for which we were all very thankful. It was the first meal we had had for several days. Indeed, for the five preceding days we had not killed as much as amounted to half a partridge for each man, and some days had not a single mouthful. While we were in this earlier state of distress, the northern Indians were by no means in want. They always walked foremost and had ten times the chance to kill partridge, rabbits, or any other thing to be met with. Besides this advantage, they had great stocks of flour, oatmeal, and other English provisions which they had swindled out of my stock during the early part of the journey."

Hearne's cool leadership was assisted by good weather. They walked out of the region of icy winds and whirling snow into a bright and serene countryside, where deer were nibbling at the bark of the trees. They found beaver in frozen streams; and willow partridge, their brown plumage now turned white for the winter, emerged daily from their burrows in the snow to feed in great numbers on the banks of every creek.

The five heavily burdened and travel-worn men sighted Prince of Wales Fort on December 8, 1769. As soon as they entered the gates in the great stone walls, Hearne had the unhappy task of telling Governor Norton that the Indian guides had run away, that they had stolen all the food they could lay their hands on, and that he had been forced to leave behind heavy loads of ammunition when he started on the return journey. In other words, his first attempt at exploration had been a miserable failure.

"A great pity, Mr. Hearne," said Governor Norton. "I am surprised that Chawchinahaw behaved so badly. I thought he was an excellent fellow. The Company in London will be none too pleased over the result of our efforts, I think, but I will have to make out a report on your journey, which will go by the first ship next spring."

"By which time I hope to be on my way to greater success," Hearne replied.

Governor Norton looked at him. "Eh? What's that, Mr. Hearne? Just what do you mean?"

"I am referring to my next journey," explained Hearne. "The Company invited me to try to reach the Coppermine River. I've failed once, but I've learned a lot. With your permission, I'm going to try again."

Chapter Four

The Second Retreat

A WANDERING party of Chipewyan Indians
had come to the fort during Hearne's absence.
They had been caught by bad weather while far
from their accustomed hunting grounds and had
been practically dying of hunger when they
staggered into the warmth and safety of the fort.
Norton had ordered them to be fed and had

given them the job of shooting partridge daily.

Hearne talked often with these northern Indians. One of them, a lean, hard-faced man with a particularly dark complexion, declared that he knew the country around the Coppermine River. "I have not seen the Far-off Metal River," he told Hearne, "but I have been within three days' journey of it. I would be willing to take you there. You were foolish to trust Chawchinahaw. I know him to be a great rogue and a man of poor courage."

Hearne looked sharply at this Indian, whose name was Connequefe. He was beginning to understand the Indian character and was not quite certain he could trust this man. Connequefe spoke easily and with much assurance, but there was doubt in Hearne's mind. He went to see the Governor.

"A very good man," said Norton, when he heard Connequefe's name. "You can trust him anywhere. We'll get two of his own Chipewyan tribe to go with him, and also a couple of our Cree Indians."

"Men with wives, of course," said Hearne.

"No, no," said Norton. "No women on this

trip, Mr. Hearne. And no other Europeans, either. Ibester is willing to go with you again, but Merriman declares he'll never make another overland journey as long as he remains in Canada. Indeed, he's not yet completely recovered from the bad cold he caught."

Hearne looked at the Governor thoughtfully. A suspicion was growing in his mind that Norton was jealous. The directors of the Hudson's Bay Company would feel very friendly toward the man who reached the Coppermine River, and Norton knew it. The Governor did not like junior officials who were on good terms with the directors in London.

"I don't mind about Ibester and Merriman," Hearne said, "but Indian women are necessary for the trip. They can haul sledges or carry loads as heavy as a man. They know how to dress skins for clothing, always pitch the tents for the men, collect firewood, and cook the food."

"No women," repeated Norton, and Hearne knew then for sure that the Governor was either jealous or else utterly ignorant of everything about Indian camp life.

He turned and walked out of the Governor's

apartments and started preparing for the journey. If Connequefe and the rest of the men were willing to travel without women, so was he.

Hearne and his five companions, with Connequefe as guide, left the fort in February, 1770. The Indians grumbled about leaving their women behind, but the rewards that Hearne promised on their return had successfully tempted them.

From what the northern Indians told him, Hearne guessed that the Coppermine River lay somewhere to the northwest of Hudson Bay. It was about all he did know, for no European had yet crossed Canada on foot. Men were still guessing how wide the continent of North America was, and there were some who believed that the Pacific Ocean was only a few days' journey from Hudson Bay. Hearne had to trust Connequefe absolutely to guide him in the right direction.

From the start of the journey, the men were handicapped by the lack of women to help carry the loads. Hearne wrote in his journal:

"Deer were so plentiful for the first eight or ten days that the Indians killed as many as was necessary; but we were all so heavy-laden that we could not possibly take much of the meat with us. This was a great evil, which exposed us to frequent inconveniences. In case of not killing anything for three or four days together, we were in great want of provisions. We seldom, however, went to bed entirely supperless till the eighth of March, when, though we had only walked about eight miles that morning and expended all the remainder of the day in hunting, we could not produce a single thing at night, not even a partridge."

Elsewhere in his journal, Hearne explains that Indian women "are able to carry loads weighing from 112 lbs. to 140 lbs. in Summer, or haul a much greater weight in Winter."

Beside a little lake somewhere on the upper reaches of the Seal River, Connequefe turned his dark face toward the sky. "We would be wise to remain here," he said, "until the geese begin to fly northward. The weather is too cold at this time for us to cross the Barren Lands to the north, and if we follow the shelter of the forest, it will take us only to the west."

Hearne approved of the suggestion. They erected their tent on a little hill beside the lake, where the shores were ringed with groves of pine, larch, birch, and poplar. Above the tops of these trees rose the white summits of the surrounding hills. When the men lay on their warm beds of pine tips inside the tent, they could hear the steady roar of a waterfall less than two hundred yards away. The swiftness of the current had prevented the water from freezing. Those late-winter and early-spring days were the most comfortable Hearne ever enjoyed during his explorations.

The moose-leather tent was made as windproof as possible by piling snow and pine tips round its outside lower edges. The entrance was to leeward for protection against the cold wind, and flaps enabled this entrance to be opened and closed. A hot little fire of pine chips burned day and night in the center of the tent. When all six men were inside, the flaps closed, and the fire burning well, the temperature was only a few degrees below freezing. And to any arctic traveler, that was real comfort.

There was little to do except catch fish in the lake through holes chopped in the ice, hunt for partridge, and perhaps shoot an occasional deer. Yet Hearne contrived to keep himself occupied

every day. Filling in his route on the blank map
he had drawn kept him busy for a while, and in
order to save ammunition, he spent the rest of
his time making traps. As a countryman he was
expert in this kind of work.

"To snare partridge requires no other process than
making a few little hedges across a creek, or a few
short hedges projecting at right angles from the
side of an island of willows, which those birds are
found to frequent. Several openings must be left
in each hedge to admit the birds to pass through,
and in each of them a snare must be set. When the
partridge are hopping along the edge of the willows
to feed, which is their usual custom, some of them
soon get into the snares. I have caught from three
to ten partridge in a day by this simple contrivance,
which requires no further attendance than going
round the snares night and morning."

Warmer weather and a brighter sun came at
the end of April. "The geese will be flying soon,"
said Connequefe, "and there will be fish and
beaver in the streams. The deer are moving out
to the Barren Grounds. There will be plenty of
food for all of us now."

Connequefe was wrong. As soon as they left
the lake behind they moved in a northwesterly

direction across a cold gray landscape that was
utterly empty of game. For five or six days
Hearne and his companions had nothing to eat
but a few cranberries. By that time a number of
northern Indians had joined their party.

> "I well knew they had had a plentiful winter,"
> said Hearne, "and had good stocks of dried meat by
> them. They knew we were in distress, but they
> never gave me or my Cree Indians the least supply,
> although in secret they provided well for our north-
> ern guides."

Hearne remembered bitterly how Moses Norton had forbidden him to take any Indian women
as load carriers and cooks. As a result of that
foolish or malicious order, there had been nothing but trouble and hunger all the way. The
instructions would have to be ignored. Hearne
was tired of eating cranberries, scraps of old
leather, and burnt bones. "See if you can get any
of the northern women to join our party," he said
to Connequefe. "We'll need about six of them
if we're to travel fast and easily."

The six women were found. Hearne's party of
twelve began to cross scrubby plains, where the

snow was soft and mushy in the heat of the June
sunshine, and geese, deer, and wild duck were
feeding beside every stream or lake. By the
tenth of June the snow had become so watery
that snowshoes and sledges were no longer of
any use. They were thrown away, and every
man and woman took a load on his back.

"This I found to be much harder work than winter
travel, as my part of the luggage consisted of the
following articles: the quadrant and its stand, a
trunk containing books, papers, etc., a land compass,
and a large bag containing all my wearing apparel;
also, a hatchet, knives, files, etc., beside several small
articles intended for presents to the natives. The
awkwardness of my load added to its weight, and
the excessive heat of the weather caused walking to
become the most laborious task I had ever come
across. What considerably increased the hardship
was the badness of the road and the coarseness of
the lodging, for the tent we had with us was not
only too large and unfit for Barren Ground service,
but we had been obliged to cut it up [cut into it]
for shoes."

The flocks of birds flew on northward and
gradually disappeared from the Barren Grounds.
Deer became scarcer and scarcer until none were

left. Stocks of meat carried by the Indian women became so putrid in the heat that even the Indians declared themselves unable to eat the stuff.

> "From the twentieth to the twenty-third of June we walked every day without any other nourishment than a pipe of tobacco and a drink of water when we pleased. Even partridge and gulls, which some time before were in great plenty and easily procured, were now so scarce and shy that we could rarely get one."

Hearne's party managed to survive. He was a lucky traveler, for somehow or other he and his companions always managed to shoot or trap some kind of game before their strength failed. This time they reached "a large lake called Yath-kyed-whoie, or White Snow Lake. Here we found several tents of northern Indians who had been some time employed spearing deer in their canoes as they crossed a little river."

The leader of these northern Indians was a short and bandy-legged fellow with remarkably small black eyes, a great hooked nose, and three horizontal black lines tattooed on each of his cheeks. He declared to Hearne that his name was Keelshies.

"I and my friends are heading for Prince of Wales Fort with furs to sell," he said. "If there is anything you need, I will bring it from the fort. Connequefe and I will agree on a meeting place where I will be able to find you."

Hearne was getting to know his Indians. Keelshies did not seem to him a man who could be trusted very far out of sight. "I will write a letter to the Governor," he said, "and ask him to give you the things to bring to me."

Hearne's letter merely asked for a little powder, shot, tobacco, and a few knives. He needed shoes, blankets, brandy, and clothing, but it seemed likely that if Keelshies ever got his hands on such goods, he would disappear quickly in the wrong direction.

With dried deermeat as reserve rations, and netting fish and shooting whatever game they could find, Hearne and his party swung westward from Yathkyed Lake (its modern name) to Dubawnt Lake. When he reached that lake, he had walked a total distance of nearly a thousand miles, for the Indians had preferred a wandering route through areas where they were likely to find game, rather than a direct line.

"The land was entirely barren and destitute of every kind of herbage except wish-a-capucca [a bitter-tasting plant which travelers sometimes used as tea] and moss. Yet the deer were so numerous that the Indians killed as many as were sufficient for our large number. Often they merely took the skins and marrow from the bones and left the carcasses to rot, or to be devoured by the wolves, foxes, and other beasts of prey."

By that time Hearne's company of travelers had grown to about six hundred northern Indian men, women, and children, so it is easy to imagine the enormous numbers of deer which roamed that empty and silent countryside.

Soon they reached the chain of rivers and lakes which flowed southwestward into the mighty Great Slave Lake. Hearne bought a small birch-bark canoe from an Indian for a small knife, which was worth, so he says, one penny. He used the unsteady little craft for ferrying his party across these rivers.

"The canoe, though of the usual size, was too small to carry more than two persons, one of whom always lies down at full length for fear of making the canoe top-heavy. The other sits on his heels and paddles."

All this travel was excellent training for Hearne. He had become an expert on snow-shoes, and his strong muscles had been tough-ened still more by long weeks of hauling a heavy sledge. He had learned where to look for game, to eat cheerfully the awful stews which the In-dian women sometimes produced as food, and to stay alive during a blizzard when he had no tent. But he had not yet become a shrewd and watchful explorer; there were still many things for him to learn. One of them was never to trust an Indian with precious belongings.

Early in August Hearne decided to go deer hunting. One of his Indians had little to carry except a leather bag of black powder. "Take my quadrant and its stand for the day," Hearne said to him. "Your load is lighter than mine."

Hearne and some Indian hunters walked about eight or nine miles. They halted on a hill-side and erected a flag as a signal to the rest of the Indians to pitch their camp there that night. All that day was spent hunting, and by sunset they were heavily burdened with fresh meat. On their return to the newly pitched tents, Hearne realized his mistake.

"I found that only part of the Indians had arrived, and that the man who had been entrusted with my powder and quadrant had set off another way with a small party of Indians. The evening being late, we were obliged to delay going in search of him till the morning. His track could not be easily discovered in the Summer, so the southern Indians, as well as myself, were very uneasy. We feared we had lost the powder which was to provide us with food and clothing for the rest of our journey. The very rude behavior of the northern Indians gave me little hope of receiving any assistance from them. During the whole time I had been with them, not one of them had offered to give me the least morsel of food without asking something in exchange."

Hearne was really in trouble. Without his quadrant, he would be unable to calculate latitudes, and unless he could do that, it would be almost impossible to draw maps. Even if the northern Indians guided him to the Coppermine River, he would be unable to locate its position accurately. It might take years of searching to find the river again.

That night Hearne was a very worried and unhappy young man. At daybreak he and the two southern Indians set off to search for the missing man. It was a hot and windless day, and the clouds of whining, biting mosquitoes were worse than ever.

All that morning, all that afternoon, they roamed back and forth across the stony ground, searching desperately for tracks left by the deserter and his friends. The sun had almost reached the western horizon when they came to a little stream. In the mud beside the bank they saw a number of footprints. And then, with tremendous relief and delight, Hearne sighted the precious quadrant and the bag of powder lying on top of a rock. Some of the powder was missing, but at least there was enough left to carry on with the northward journey.

For another five days, the straggling mass of Indians wandered on across the plains, always noisy, always in search of something to eat, usually talking or squabbling among themselves in loud and strident voices. No wonder that Hearne's journal grew daily more bitter. Long ago he had decided that these northern Indians were the worst companions one could have on a journey, and probably the world's rudest savages.

Then came the disaster which brought

Hearne's second journey to an end some twelve hundred miles from the fort.

"*August 12, 1770.* It proving rather cloudy about noon, though very fine weather, I left the quadrant standing (on its spindly three-legged tripod) while I was eating my dinner. A sudden gust of wind blew it down; and as the ground where it stood was very rocky, the bubble, the sight vane, and vernier were entirely broken to pieces. This rendered the instrument useless. As a result of this misfortune I resolved to return again to the Fort."

Perhaps Hearne's only consolation was the thought that he had succeeded in traveling through hundreds of miles of country never previously reached by any European, and that he had almost entered the Arctic Circle.

Chapter Five

A Friendly Indian

CONNEQUEFE and the other four Indians, particularly the two Cree, were delighted to be going south again. Like most primitive people who become familiar with European customs, they no longer enjoyed their old way of life. They much preferred a warm bed at the fort, food out of barrels, and a helping of brandy whenever they could get it.

Even after Hearne and his five companions

had parted from the horde of northern Indians, those wretched savages brought fresh misfortune to him. He was sitting in his tent when a gang of seven Chipewyans entered the camp. They were carrying tomahawks, bows, and knives, and appeared a really villainous crowd. Their ringleader sat down beside Hearne, and the rest of them sprawled inside the tent.

"Give me *skipertogan*," said the leader. "We need to fill our pipes."

Hearne handed over the neat little leather bag, ornamented with beads, in which he kept his tobacco and pipe. There was nothing else he could do.

The Chipewyans sat and smoked in silence for a while, passing the *skipertogan* from one to another. "Give us blankets," said the leader. "Also an iron cooking pot and some fishhooks."

"I have none," Hearne replied.

The Indians looked at him with disgust. "You are indeed a very poor man. If we went to the fort we would be given many presents by rich white men. Some cards, then, and knives."

"I have no knives to spare and not a single pack of cards," said Hearne.

Another Indian reached out a hand and touched the leather bag in which Hearne kept his belongings. "Yours?" he asked.

Hearne nodded. He knew what was coming, but there was nothing he could do to avoid it.

"The Indian and the rest of his companions soon had all my treasures spread on the ground. One took one thing, and another took something else, till at last nothing was left but the empty bag, which they permitted me to keep. At length, considering that, though I was going to the Factory, I should need a knife to cut my food, an awl to mend my shoes, and a needle to mend my other clothing, they readily gave me these articles, though not without making me understand that I ought to look upon it as a great favor.

"Seeing they were being so generous (!) I ventured to ask them for my razors. Thinking that one would be sufficient to shave me during the passage home, they kept the other; luckily they chose the worst. To complete their generosity, they permitted me to take as much soap as I thought would be sufficient to wash and shave me during my journey to the Fort."

Having looted Hearne, the Chipewyans left the tent and proceeded to steal everything belonging to the Cree. These two Indians were

left with nothing except their guns, some ammunition, an old ax, an ice chisel, and a file.

Connequefe was a northern Indian, but his
fellow countrymen had little use for him. They
examined his possessions, took what they liked,
and left him little better off than Hearne and the
two Cree.

Hearne led his party eastward as fast as he
could. September had come, and frost was yel-
lowing the leaves. Across the cold blue sky the
first flocks of birds were migrating south. There
was no chance of reaching the fort before November, and early winter was no time to be
traveling overland without proper supplies of
clothing and ammunition.

The Indian who was to become Hearne's best
friend appeared from the west. He came walking across the low hills, followed by thirty or
forty Chipewyan warriors and some women, all
of whom were carrying packs of fur. His name
was Matonabi, and he and his party were going
to Prince of Wales Fort to trade their beaver and
marten skins.

Matonabi was about thirty-five years old and
almost six feet in height. He had a dark-skinned,

handsome face, and it was not disfigured by the three or four black lines that the other northern Indians tattooed on their cheeks. Whereas most of the Chipewyans were sour-looking, harsh-featured people, Matonabi had a cheerful and friendly face.

"Why do you wear such thin clothing?" Matonabi asked Hearne. "Only madmen would travel as you are doing. Do you wish to die of cold? Why have you no snowshoes or sledges?"

"Your tribe, the Chipewyans, took most of what we had," replied Hearne. "We cannot make snowshoes, because there is no wood for the frames in these Barren Lands."

"If my people took your things from you," said Matonabi, "it is only proper that I should give you other things to replace them. I lived at your fort for several years and shot partridge for your people. Your Governor, Moses Norton, knows me very well. I see you have a few deer-skins with you. Let me have them, and our women will make warm clothes for you. Ten skins are needed to make a good suit, but my men can supply the rest. Snowshoes I cannot give you. But tomorrow I will guide you to a little patch of trees where you can get wood to make sledges and snowshoes for yourselves."

Matonabi kept his word. Wearing warm and heavy clothing, with new, well-made snowshoes on their feet, Hearne and his five men traveled southward with Matonabi's party at a rate of ten or twelve miles daily. Now there was no need for them to worry about where their next meal was coming from. The men in Matonabi's party were good hunters, and they brought back freshly killed deer to the camp every day.

"Will you make another journey?" Matonabi asked Hearne, as they sat by the glowing fire in their tent one evening. "Or have you grown weary of trying to reach the Far-off Metal River?"

"I will try again," Hearne replied. "I have made mistakes in the past through ignorance, and sometimes carelessness, but now I have learned how a northern journey should be made. There will be Indian women in the next party I lead."

Matonabi's teeth gleamed in the firelight as he laughed. "Your Governor was wrong in not letting women go with you this time. When the men are carrying heavy loads, they can neither hunt nor travel very far. If they kill deer, who is to carry the meat? Women are made to work. One of them can carry or haul as much as two men can, yet it costs little to feed them. As they always cook the food, they can live by licking their fingers when game is scarce. So I say to you, my friend, that you are right to insist that women travel with you when you come northward again. And I say this to you also: let me be your guide for the third journey, and you will find less hardship and hunger than you have known up to the present."

"If the Governor agrees," said Hearne, "you will certainly be the man who goes with me. I know that I can trust you, and because you are a northern Indian your countrymen will be less anxious to rob me on every occasion."

Hearne arrived at Prince of Wales Fort on November 25, 1770, after having been away for about nine months. He had failed to reach the unknown northern coast, but in his stout leather bag were careful, well-drawn maps of regions which no other European had ever visited.

When those same maps reached England,

geographers hastened to examine them. They nodded their heads approvingly. "Here at last," they said, "is a man with the courage it takes to reach the arctic wilderness on foot. A man, also, who can fill in latitudes and longitudes, and draw charts as neatly as our best draftsmen."

Governor Norton had not changed his peculiar ideas concerning the proper way for Hearne to travel overland. "You can make another journey if you wish," he said, "and there is no reason why Matonabi should not act as your guide. Tell him to choose some of our Cree Indians to go with you."

"No," said Hearne. "Not one single Cree goes with me on my next trip."

Something had happened to Samuel Hearne in those white, wind-swept wastes northwest of the Churchill River. He had starved so often, and had been disappointed so many times, that he was no longer the same quiet young man who had once been content to keep pets in his sitting room and draw handsome sketches of the fort. His blue eyes had developed a very hard expression, and there was a look of severity on his face. He was thinner nowadays, and he seemed to appear even taller.

"No Cree?" inquired Governor Norton, a little uncertainly. "There are many excellent men in the tribe, and you'd be lost without their help."

Norton was half Cree himself, and Hearne knew it. But that did not affect his next remark. "They've been of precious little use to me up to the present," he said. "They've been spoiled by easy living here at the fort. They don't know how to hunt, they're hopelessly lazy, and the Chipewyan Indians up north despise them. Besides which, they're utter thieves. I will not take any of them with me. However, I do propose taking a number of women, as well as some of Matonabi's Chipewyans."

Moses Norton never forgave Hearne for his remarks.

"I offended Mr. Norton to such a degree that neither time nor absence could ever afterwards remove his dislike of me. After my return he used every means in his power to treat me ill and to render my life unhappy. However, to be honest, it must be acknowledged to his honor he did not allow our argument to interfere with private business. I was fitted out with ammunition and every other article which Matonabi thought could be wanted. I was also equipped, as before, with a small assortment of light trading goods as presents to the far-distant Indians."

The third journey began on December 7, 1770. Hearne, with his mixed party of Chipewyan men and women, was starting north again only twelve days after the end of the second expedition. Quadrants were naturally somewhat scarce in the Company's stores. The one which Hearne now carried he described a little coldly as "an old instrument which had been upwards of thirty years at the Fort."

Chapter Six

The Ways of an Indian Chief

MATONABI had no wish to wander along slowly, as Hearne's previous guides had done. The weather was so cold now that sledges moved easily across the frozen snow. At a rate of sixteen or eighteen miles daily, they moved northward along the familiar route toward Seal

River and then swung westward toward Great
Slave Lake. There were good hunters in the
party, and they traveled light, the women hauling the ponderous sledges. Except for a few
days at Christmas time, when, as he wrote, "We
did not taste a morsel of anything, except a pipe
of tobacco and a drink of snow water," Hearne
ate better and was looked after more carefully
than ever before.

Matonabi himself had no intention of lacking
any possible comfort during the journey. He
had brought his six wives with him, and they
were accustomed to doing all the work while on
the march.

> "Most of them would, for size, have made good
> grenadiers," wrote Hearne. "Matonabi prided him-
> self much in the height and strength of his wives,
> and would often say few women would carry or haul
> heavier loads. Though these women had, in general,
> a very masculine appearance, yet he preferred them
> to those of a more delicate form and moderate
> stature. . . . Take them in a body, the [Indian]
> women are as lacking real beauty as any nation I
> ever saw. There are some few of them, when young,
> who are passable, but the care of a family, added to
> their constant hard labor, soon makes the most beau-

tiful among them look old and wrinkled even before they are thirty. . . . Ask a northern Indian, 'What is beauty?' He will answer, 'A broad, flat face, small eyes, high cheekbones, three or four broad black lines across each cheek, a low forehead, a large broad chin, a clumsy hooknose, and a tawny skin.' "

Besides liking comfort, Matonabi was an unusually gluttonous eater, even for an Indian. At the end of December, after being on short rations for a few days, the hunters brought in some deer. Matonabi surprised even Hearne by the enormous size of the meal he ate that evening. The next day he was feeling very ill.

"I am going to die," he told Hearne. "Now I will never be able to guide you to the Far-off Metal River. You will have to go back to the fort."

"You are not going to die," Hearne replied. "Your stomach is sore because you ate too much."

"That is foolish talk," the chief replied. "Even animals know when they have had enough to eat."

"The black bear doesn't," Hearne replied. "In the summer, when the berries are ripe, he eats so many that he vomits up great quantities of them and immediately begins devouring more."

Matonabi grunted and looked at Hearne in a surprised manner. Next morning he was still so ill that he had to be hauled on a sledge by one of his wives. All that day, however, he refrained from eating anything. He was better when camp was pitched that night, and by the following morning he was able to walk again.

Early in March, 1771, Hearne reached the Dubawnt River. From then on, his journal became full of strange Indian names for the various places they passed through: Whold-yeah'd Whoie (Pike Lake), Thelewey-aza-yeth (Little Fish Hill), Tittameg Lake, and Scartack Lake. In Matonabi's well-run camp, Hearne did not have to spend most of his days hunting for food, persuading the Indians not to desert, or preventing them from stealing his stocks of food and ammunition. He had time to prepare new maps, so beautifully drawn and carefully inscribed that no later traveler who used them would ever lose his way.

Far west of the Dubawnt River, more Indians on their way north joined Hearne's party. Their numbers varied daily, some lingering at a spot where the fishing or hunting was unusually good, others turning their backs upon a region where they had found little to eat.

Early in May, Matonabi decided to halt for a few days. "A land of rivers and lakes lies to the northward," he told Hearne. "We are heading in that direction, and we will need canoes to cross the streams. Those trees yonder are the last we will see for many hundreds of miles."

The only tools used by the Indians in making their canoes were a hatchet, a knife, a file, and an awl. Yet so clever were they with these tools that the canoes they made could not have been neater if they had worked with every tool in a carpenter's shop.

"In shape the northern Indian canoe is flat-bottomed, with straight upright sides and sharp at each end. The stern is by far the widest part, as there the baggage is generally laid, and occasionally a second person, who always lies down at full length in the bottom of the canoe. In this manner they carry one another across rivers and the narrow parts of lakes in those little vessels, which seldom exceed twelve or thirteen feet in length and are from twenty inches to two feet broad in the widest part."

The canoes were made and tested in a lake which lay close to the camp. Just about that time Matonabi, perhaps thinking that he had not enough wives for a man of his importance, went to another man's tent and took away his wife. It was the usual custom among these northern Indians for the strongest men and the most expert hunters to have more wives than the smaller and weaker men. Matonabi was a chief and considered himself perfectly free to take someone else's wife whenever he chose. But this particular girl, according to Hearne, was "of a moderate size and had a fair complexion. She possessed a mild temper and very engaging manners. In fact, she seemed to have every good quality that could be expected of a northern Indian woman."

Quite naturally, the girl's husband objected to her removal. He spoke rudely to Matonabi, thereby causing the chief to fall into a silent and sulky mood which lasted for several days.

One night Matonabi opened his baggage, took out a new long-bladed knife, went into the man's tent, and stabbed him three times. Luckily, the wounds were all on the shoulder blade. The warriors who ran to the spot saved the man from death and persuaded Matonabi to return to his tent.

"Was I not perfectly right to stab that man?" asked the chief, as he washed the blood off his hands. "The fellow was angry merely because I brought his wife to live in my tent."

"The Europeans have different customs," Hearne replied. "But if one of us takes another man's wife, there is always trouble." He did not add that it was the European who lost his wife who made the trouble. Hearne was very anxious to avoid upsetting the chief by criticizing him in any way.

Matonabi grunted disapprovingly. "Women are not worth arguing about. What difference does one more or less of them make to a man?"

A few days later, Matonabi changed his views on this subject. His new wife ran off in the middle of the night, accompanied by another woman. He searched for them the next day but without success. "It was supposed," wrote Hearne, "that they went off to the eastward to meet their former husbands, from whom they had been sometime before taken by force."

While Matonabi was still in a bad temper over his loss, a powerful young warrior visited him in his tent. "O Matonabi," he said, "I have come to wrestle with you in the usual manner for one of your wives. It is White Marten, who is so clever at making garments from leather and furs."

According to the northern Indian custom, any man could challenge another, even a chief, to wrestle with him for the possession of a wife. The man who won took the woman.

"I am in no mood for wrestling today," Matonabi replied in a surly voice. "My head is troubled by many thoughts."

What Matonabi really meant—and Hearne knew it—was that he did not want to risk losing another wife. Matonabi was a strong man, but the visiting warrior was younger and probably more powerful.

"Then let us settle the matter another way," said the Indian politely. "Give me some powder and lead, a new knife, an awl, and a file. Also a kettle, some thread, and eight needles. Then we will talk no more about wrestling for your woman."

Hearne, who was listening to this conversation, grinned to himself. He liked Matonabi, who was the best Indian he had met, but he also remembered how the chief had behaved only a few days earlier.

"But I bought White Marten from you only a couple of months ago," Matonabi complained angrily. "I gave you much ironware for her at the time."

"All of which I have given away as presents to others," the warrior answered. "And I see now that I was wrong to sell so clever and industrious a wife. But if you do not wish to give me more ironware, then come. Let us wrestle outside your tent."

The argument lasted several hours. The result was that Matonabi handed over the articles the warrior demanded, and kept his wife.

"This dispute was likely to have proved fatal to my expedition. Matonabi, who at that time thought himself as great a man as then lived, took this insult so much to heart, especially as it was offered in my presence, that he almost determined not to proceed any farther toward the Coppermine River. He was

on the point of striking off to the Westward to join
the Athabascan Indians and live with them. He was
friendly with all their leaders and most of the prin-
cipal Indians of that country, from whom, he said,
he had met with more civility than he ever did from
his countrymen."

Hearne spent an entire day arguing with
Matonabi. Late in the evening, the chief appeared to be in a better humor and agreed to
remain with the expedition.

The next day Keelshies, the bandy-legged
little Indian whom Hearne had met on his last
expedition, walked into the camp. He had taken
the letter from Hearne to the fort and now had
at last returned.

"I have brought you a packet of letters and a
two-quart keg of brandy," he said. "The
Governor also gave me powder, shot, tobacco,
knives, and blankets to bring to you. But during the past winter some of my family died,
and according to our Indian custom, I was
obliged to throw away everything that belonged
to me. After that, I had to use the things that
were meant for you to feed and clothe my wives
and family."

At this point Keelshies began to howl loudly. Hearne, who was getting to know the Indians by this time, was not surprised by the little rogue's tears. Indians were able to weep whenever they chose, pausing to draw at a pipe of tobacco or to speak to a friend, then proceeding with their noisy crying. Hearne, although surprised by Keelshies' return, was certain that the Indian was a villain.

Day after day the straggling crowd of Indians, which now numbered four or five hundred, continued to move northward across the snow-covered Barren Lands. While the women plodded along, hauling heavy sledges behind them, the men circled on the flanks of the untidy procession in search of game. Sometimes they found deer in the shelter of patchy groves of twisted and stunted pine. There were fish in the rocky streams and lakes which lay like black lines and patches across the pure whiteness of the desolate plain. Long before nightfall, a site for the camp was chosen. Tent poles and moose-leather coverings were unstrapped from the sledges, deer were skinned and prepared for cooking, and small fires began to burn brightly inside the seventy or eighty tents. As soon as darkness came, and reflected starlight glittered on the snow, the Indians wrapped themselves in their sleeping robes, carefully built up the fires, and lay down to sleep until the cold gray light of early morning.

But the farther northward they went, the shorter became the nights. When they camped beside a small patch of water which the Indians called Peshew Lake, the darkness was intense for only an hour or two near midnight. It was nearly the end of May in the year 1771, and Hearne knew that he had almost reached the Arctic Circle. There, during the summer months, the sun would not set at all.

"We must leave most of the women and all the children behind if we are to reach the Coppermine River this summer," Matonabi said. "Men can travel fast by themselves if they have only light loads and sufficient supplies of dried meat. We will leave our women in camp here until we return from the North. There are fish and beaver in the lake, so they will be able to feed themselves while we are gone. But I will take with me two young wives who have no children and will be useful for cooking food and attending to other work."

On May 31, 1771, Hearne started the last part of his journey into the Arctic Circle. As the warriors, some sixty in number, plodded off on their snowshoes across the white plain, the women and children left behind "set up a most woeful cry, and continued to yell most piteously as long as we were within hearing."

But the northern Indians, as Hearne had already noticed a long time ago, had no affection for their wives and very little for their own children. He was not surprised that the warriors did not even turn their heads to look back at the camp, and merely laughed at the noise made by the grieving women.

Hearne saw that the Indians were now carrying shields made of wood that they had collected from a few straggly trees growing round Peshew Lake. These shields were nearly an inch thick, two feet wide, and about three feet long.

"We have heard that there is a party of Eskimos camping beside the Coppermine River," Matonabi said calmly. "We learned the news from the Copper Indians, who live far to the north of here. Three of their hunters came to our camp a few days ago. We will need the shields when we attack the Eskimos."

"Why do you want to attack them?" asked Hearne. "They have done you no harm."

"They are Eskimos," Matonabi replied. "We always kill them when we see them."

During the past months Hearne had become familiar with the utterly savage ways of his Indian companions. He had even seen some of them beat their wives until the unhappy women died. Hearne loathed their extraordinary cruelty, for he was a goodhearted and kindly person, always eager to be friendly toward others. This intended attack on the Eskimos shocked him greatly. Even though his very life depended on remaining friends with the Chipewyan Indians, he was courageous enough to open his mouth now and say exactly what he thought. As he must have known would happen, his words only caused trouble.

"I tried as much as possible to persuade them from carrying out their inhuman idea, but so far were my entreaties from having the wished-for effect, that it was believed I spoke from cowardice. The Indians told me with great signs of scorn that I was afraid of the Eskimos. As I knew my personal safety depended on the favorable opinion they held of me in this respect, I was obliged to change my tone. I replied that I did not care if they rendered the name and race of the Eskimos extinct. I added at the same time, though, that I was no enemy to the Eskimos and did not see the necessity of attacking them without cause."

Hearne and his party were now crossing the most bleak frozen plain he had ever seen. Streams and lakes were encased in heavy ice, across which the bitter wind sent flurries of snow dancing and whirling. The cold was bearable in the daytime, when the temperature was only fifteen or twenty degrees below freezing point, but at night it became really frightful. The men lay on moss at the bottom of holes which they had scraped in the snow, covered themselves with a single deerskin, and hungrily gnawed frozen deermeat. From their earliest childhood the Indians had been accustomed to the hardship of frigid northern winters, but it was a miracle that Samuel Hearne, an Englishman, managed to survive.

On June 21, Hearne wrote a brief paragraph
in his journal, which recorded his great achieve-
ment as an explorer.

"We had bad rainy weather, with so thick a fog
that we could not see our way. About ten o'clock
at night, however, it became fine and clear, and the
sun shone very bright; indeed, it did not set all that
night. This was a convincing proof that we were
then considerably to the North of the Arctic Polar
Circle."

After six months of exhausting travel, Hearne
had become the first white man to reach the
Arctic Circle on foot.

The party encountered Copper Indians a few
days later. They were taller than the northern
Indians, and many of them were six feet in
height. They had heavy, coppery-brown faces,
low foreheads, and long braids of black hair.
Their plump cheeks were tattooed with horizontal black lines, like those of the northern
Indians, but their bodies and faces were
strangely hairless. Their manners were reasonably good, and Hearne soon noticed that these
Copper Indians, not having been spoiled by the
Europeans at the trading posts, which they

never visited, did not spend their time cadging or whining or making threats in order to get presents. With even greater relief, Hearne also noticed that the Copper Indians were reasonably clean and "as free from an offensive smell as any of the human race."

The Copper Indians, never having seen a white man before, were just as interested in Hearne as he was in them. They grinned and shuffled their feet with pleasure when he distributed small presents among them: a few fishhooks, an awl or two, and a little knife for the headman. Afterward they formed a ring and stared long and attentively at the big, burly figure in worn deerskins.

"He is a man just like us," they declared, "except that his yellow hair is like that on the end of a buffalo's tail. Also, his eyes are of a curious color such as is never seen among ordinary men. They are more like those of a gull. His skin is ugly, for it is like meat which has lain too long in water."

The meeting between Copper and northern Indians occurred at a place with the impossible name of Cong-e-cath-wha-chaga, which was nothing more than a few leather tents beside a frozen stream. A single campfire burned precious firewood gathered from miles around. Matonabi decided to leave the remaining women there while the warriors went forward against the Eskimos. Oddly enough, some twenty or thirty Copper Indians decided to join the war party. Their tribe had been treated badly by Hearne's northern Indians, so there was no reason at all why they should have wished to help their unpleasant guests.

"The northern Indians not only took many of the Copper tribe's young women, furs, and ready-dressed skins for clothing, but also several of their bows and arrows, which were all the Copper Indians had to procure food and clothing for the future support of themselves, their wives, and families. To do Matonabi justice on this occasion, I must say that he tried as much as possible to persuade his countrymen from taking either furs, clothing, or bows from the Copper Indians without making some satisfactory return."

After spending several days building up supplies of deermeat, the war party set off on its bloodthirsty journey. The warriors carried little besides their weapons, one blanket each, and a supply of food. Hearne alone traveled fully laden. He no longer risked entrusting his belongings to anyone except himself, and in any event the northern Indians would not, at the present time, have helped him to carry his load. Since they were out for murder they were not interested in anyone or anything else.

Chapter Seven

Death to the Eskimos

THE way to the Coppermine River lay across wild, desolate country, where only a few granite-topped hills interrupted the dreary white line of the horizon. It was the beginning of July, but Hearne was now far north of the Arctic Circle, and the polar cold lay heavy on the countryside.

"On the fourth of July we had constant light snow, which made it very disagreeable underfoot. We nevertheless walked twenty-seven miles to the Northwest, fourteen of which were on what the Indians call the Stony Mountains; and surely no part of the world better deserves that name. On our first approaching these mountains, they appeared to be a confused heap of stones, utterly inaccessible to the foot of man, but having some Copper Indians with us who knew the best road, we made fair progress, though not without being obliged to crawl on our hands and knees. By the side of the path there are, in different parts, several large flat, or table, stones, which are covered with many thousands of small pebbles. These, the Copper Indians say, have been greatly increased by passengers going to and from the mines. . . .

"Just as we arrived at the foot of the Stony Mountains, three of the Copper Indians turned back. They said that from every appearance the remainder of the journey seemed likely to be so troublesome that not even the pleasure of going to war with the Eskimos made it worthwhile."

Hearne, stooping under his heavy pack, tramped onward through icy fog and snow, sleet, and rain. His clothes had been soaked since the day he left Cong-e-cath-wha-chaga. There was no hot food of any kind, and all he had to eat was frozen deermeat. At night he and his companions usually slept in caves.

"The best were but damp and unwholesome lodging. In some the water was constantly dropping from the rock that formed the roof, which made our place of retreat little better than the open air. We had not been able to make a fire—except a spark to light a pipe—since the day we left the remainder of the women behind. In some places there was a little moss, but the constant sleet and rain made it so wet that it was impossible to set fire to."

And yet Hearne still found time to note down latitudes in his journal, to go on drawing his map on damp and moldy parchment, and to write brief but accurate descriptions of the lifeless and awful country through which they were passing. Most surprising of all, he still managed to stay alive, under conditions which would have brought pneumonia and death to the great majority of Europeans. Even some of the Indians found the going too hard. Fifteen more of them turned back to Cong-e-cath-wha-chaga, declaring they were sick and tired of this terrible journey.

After traveling for several days, Hearne saw low gray hills looming up across the northeast horizon. Snow ceased falling, the cruel wind dropped, and the sun appeared in a clear sky.

The straggling party walked more swiftly, their snowshoes creaking on the frozen surface of the snow.

Matonabi raised a deerskin-covered arm and pointed to the distant hills. "The Copper Indians say that is where the Far-off Metal River flows. They also say that on its banks stand fine groves of pine trees, where deer are plentiful. Tomorrow night we will sleep by a good fire, after eating as much roasted flesh as our stomachs can hold."

Two days later, Hearne came down from the hills to stand on the banks of a stream. He had reached the Coppermine River some forty miles above its mouth, after a journey lasting from December, 1770, until July, 1771. During those seven months he had walked more than two thousand miles, often hungry, usually cold, and nearly always tired. He deserved a reward far greater than the one he actually received as he gazed at the cold green waters of the Coppermine River.

"I was not a little surprised to find that the river differed so much from the description which the Indians had given of it at the Factory. Instead of being so large as to be navigable for shipping, it was at that part scarcely navigable for an Indian canoe. It was not more than one hundred and eighty yards wide, everywhere full of shoals, and no less than three falls were in sight at first view."

There was a chance that as the river neared the sea it might become deep and wide enough for the Company's ships to use as a waterway. During the next two days, while Indian scouts crept along the banks in search of the Eskimos, Hearne walked a distance of twenty miles down the stream. The scattered pine forest was left behind. Low hills and wide marshes surrounded him on all sides, but there was no sign of the river's becoming any better. He came to a few deep channels between the rocks, where a ship of considerable size might float easily, but these stretches of open water always ended in another rapid.

The war party came to meet Hearne at the end of his second day's journey. "Our scouts have found the Eskimo camp," they told him. "Twelve of their tents stand on the east side of the river, a few miles farther downstream. Stop looking at this river and come with us."

That night the warriors were busy painting the front of their shields with crude red-and-black drawings of the sun, the moon, devils, ghosts, or whatever else they depended on for success in the coming attack. Very early in the morning, the war party began its cautious advance toward the Eskimo camp, taking care to avoid appearing on the sky line of any hills, and speaking only in whispers. For mile after mile they waded through half-frozen swamps, which Hearne could never have crossed if he had not left most of his belongings at the camp farther upstream.

"My party, though an undisciplined rabble and by no means accustomed to war or command, acted on this horrid occasion with remarkable discipline. There was not the least argument or separate opinion. All were united in the general cause and ready to follow where Matonabi led. He, in turn, followed the advice of an old Copper Indian who had joined us on our first arrival at the river."

High above the heads of the carefully moving war party flew owl-like alarm birds, or birds of warning. These birds had the curious habit of hovering above a party of travelers, or else flying on ahead and then returning. If they saw a second party of travelers approaching the first, they made a loud screaming noise which sounded almost like a child crying. Now, as the war party drew near the Eskimo camp, the alarm birds started flying back and forth, uttering their warning noises. Unfortunately, the poor Eskimos were asleep and did not hear the warning.

Hearne caught sight of the Eskimo camp at a distance of about two hundred yards. Twelve circular tents made of deerskins stood on a patch of level stony ground near a roaring little waterfall. From the crosspiece of high wooden posts dangled strings of freshly caught salmon. Beside each tent lay a small canoe and a sledge, and a number of bushy-haired dogs were tethered to rocks, with leather thongs. There was no sign of the Eskimos, for they were still asleep inside their tents.

One of the Indians offered a spear to Hearne, and another handed him a steel-bladed bayonet. A third Indian held out a shield. Hearne shook his head. "I will go with you when you attack," he said, "for if I remain here alone, some of the

Eskimos—if any escape—may think I am an enemy of theirs and try to kill me. But I do not want your weapons. I have no wish to help in the murdering of these people."

The Indians nodded and grunted. They had always regarded Hearne as a queer fellow, because he disliked slaughtering deer for the sake of the sport, and because he showed anger when wounded animals were not killed at once. Probably they now decided he was utterly mad because he did not want to attack the Eskimos.

Hidden among the rocks and hills overlooking the camp, the Indians made final preparations for their attack.

"These chiefly consisted in painting their faces: some all black, some all red, and others with a mixture of the two. To prevent their hair from blowing into their eyes, it was either tied before and behind and on both sides, or else cut short all round. They made themselves as light as possible for running by pulling off their stockings, and either cutting off the sleeves of their jackets or rolling them up close to their armpits. Though the mosquitoes were in unbelievable numbers, some of the Indians actually pulled off their jackets and entered the battle quite naked except for their breechclouts and shoes. Fearing I might have to run with the rest, I thought it advisable to pull off my stockings and cap, and to tie my hair as close up as possible."

Led by Matonabi, the sixty warriors stood up and began to charge down the snow-covered rocky incline. They made no noise as they ran toward the camp. The dogs stared in bewilderment at the oncoming figures and barked with alarm, but the sleeping Eskimos were awakened by the noise too late. Most of them were killed inside their tents; the rest were stabbed to death as they fled toward the stream. Twenty Eskimos died that morning in their camp beside the Coppermine River. One of them, a young girl about eighteen years old, crouched almost at Hearne's feet. He pleaded vainly with the Indians to spare her life, but they jeered at him as they raised their spears.

"Do you want her as your wife?" they asked. "Are there not enough Indian girls for you to choose from?" The warriors forced Hearne aside and struck her with their spears.

"Even at this hour," Hearne wrote many years later, "I cannot think of what happened that day without shedding tears."

The Indians now sighted another camp, of

seven tents, on the opposite side of the river. These Eskimos had been awakened by the noise and were standing at the edge of the water, grasping their spears and knives. The Indians had left their canoes at their camp, farther upstream, and they had no way of crossing the eighty-yard-wide river except by swimming the icy current. Picking up the few muskets they had brought with them, they started trying to shoot their enemies.

The light muskets bought from the Hudson's Bay Company could not be fired accurately at a range of eighty yards. This fact saved the lives of the wretched Eskimos, who were so ignorant of firearms that they ran eagerly to examine every mark left by a bullet striking the ground. One of them was at last hit in the leg with a bullet, whereupon the whole party launched their canoes and paddled down the river.

The Indians turned their attention to looting the Eskimo camp. They ripped and smashed the tents, tore down the strings of drying salmon, and seized all the copper utensils, such as hatchets and knives, that they could find. They turned loose the fine Huskies, which, howling mournfully, trotted down the riverbank after the departing Eskimo canoes. Having done all the damage they could, the warriors kindled a fire with the moss fuel used by the Eskimos and cooked an enormous meal of freshly killed salmon for themselves.

"We have finished our work now," they told Hearne. "If you want to go on looking at this river and making marks and lines on paper, we are ready to help you."

They trudged northward beside the river, toward the distant sea. With every step he took, Hearne became more sure that the Coppermine was of no use to shipping. The river ran noisily over rocky projecting shoals, or leapt with an unending roar over low waterfalls. In some places it narrowed to a width of not more than twenty yards; in others it widened to four hundred.

At one o'clock on the night of July 17, Hearne and his Indians reached the sea. The polar sun was shining brightly, high above the horizon. Hearne stood on a flat rock-strewn shore and gazed northward through his small pocket telescope, while arctic gulls, curlew, and wild geese wheeled and hovered in uneasy flight above his head.

The ice had melted near the shore, and a channel of open water, nearly a mile wide, ran along the coast. But farther out to sea a great and almost unbroken ice field glittered and sparkled in the sunlight. Its white mass stretched to the horizon in every direction, and snow-covered blocks of ice, broken away from this main field, swayed and dipped across the bright blue surface of the open channel.

"So much for the Northwest Passage," Hearne said to himself. "There's ice all the way clear to the Pole. No ship will ever sail through these waters to reach the Pacific Ocean. That's the answer to a question all Europe has been asking, for over two hundred years."

Chapter Eight

The Homeward Trail

HEARNE and his Indians returned upstream to their camp. The short arctic summer was passing swiftly, and the Chipewyan Indians were anxious to head south before the autumn cold arrived. But there was something else for Hearne to do before he began his homeward journey. The Company had asked him to inspect the copper mines which the Indians spoke about so often. Even though the Coppermine

River was useless for navigation, and the ore could never be shipped from there, Hearne was determined to carry out his last remaining order. He started off on a thirty-mile journey from the camp to the nearest mine, accompanied by a mixed party of northern and Copper Indians.

Disappointment awaited him again, beside a fierce little river which ran swiftly between banks of rocks and gravel.

"This is one of our best mines," the Indians told him. "By searching along these shores, a man can pick up lumps of pure copper."

But the Indians were exaggerating, as they often did when they understood the kind of answer the Europeans wanted to hear. Those who had visited the fort and been asked about the copper deposits saw that the white men were interested in finding large supplies of ore. By telling enormous lies about the quantity of copper, they made them happy and received many good presents for themselves. According to their way of thinking, they did no harm to anyone. Perhaps it never occurred to them that some European might set off to search for the copper.

"The Indians who were the reason for my making this journey declared that the mine was so rich and valuable that if a factory [warehouse] were built at the river, a ship might be ballasted with the ore instead of stone. Judging by what they said, the hills were entirely composed of the metal, all in handy lumps, like a heap of pebbles. But their story was so far from the truth that I and almost all my companions spent nearly four hours in search of some of this metal. Among the lot of us, only one piece of any size could be found. This, however, was remarkably good and weighed above four pounds." [This lump of copper is now in the British Museum in London.]

The journey back to Cong-e-cath-wha-chaga began on July 22, 1771. The Indians were anxious to travel as fast as possible, for they were growing tired of this hard trip. They were eager to smell good meat roasting over campfires, to lie down in their tents and wrap warm buffalo robes around their bodies. On the first day of their return journey they walked forty-two miles and reached the grim wind-swept passes of the Stony Mountains. The next day they walked twenty-seven miles, and the day after that, thirty-one miles.

When the Indians came to their camp at Cong-e-cath-wha-chaga, they grunted loudly with dismay. It was deserted, except for an old Indian and his family.

"Your wives and children decided to start moving south," this Indian told Hearne's party. "The fish in the stream were not enough to feed them all after some of the Copper Indians came back, and the deer have moved away from this region."

"Then we will follow them at once," the Indians declared, and pointed to a pillar of white smoke rising up against the distant southern sky. "Yonder are our women, making a signal for us. We will sleep in our own tents tonight."

With precious little thought for Hearne, who was still carrying a heavy load on his shoulders, the Indians started walking swiftly toward the column of smoke. They had covered a hundred miles in three days across rocky hillsides, through frozen marshes, and along the winding, slippery passes of the Stony Mountains. Hearne had to keep up with them or be left behind. He knew that when an Indian fell sick on the road, his companions seldom waited for him to recover. Usually they left him with his weapons, a blanket, and such food as they could spare, and told him what direction they were taking. If the man became better, he was sometimes able to overtake them in a few days. More often, however, he died miserably on the lonely plains. Even Matonabi, who usually did his best to care for Hearne, was as eager as his warriors to reach the camp.

"From our leaving the Coppermine River to this time, we had traveled so hard and taken so little rest on the way, that my feet and legs had swelled considerably and become stiff at the ankles. I had so little power to direct my feet when walking, that I frequently knocked them against the stones with such force that my legs were badly jarred. The nails of my toes were bruised to such an extent that several of them festered and dropped off. To add to this mishap, the skin was entirely chafed off between every toe, so that the sand and gravel, which were impossible to keep out, irritated the raw parts very much. For a whole day before we arrived at the women's tents, I left the print of my feet in blood at almost every step I took. Several of the Indians began to complain that their feet also were sore, but not one of them was the twentieth part in so bad a state as mine."

The column of smoke that Hearne's party had seen from Cong-e-cath-wha-chaga came from smoldering moss. The women, who had left the place four days ago, had set the moss alight as a signal. By this time even the youngest warriors were exhausted, and the whole party camped on the deserted site. Next morning Hearne could scarcely stand up, and his first few steps were so agonizing that he groaned with pain.

Another column of smoke was rising in the southern sky, and the Indians headed toward it.

They walked from seven in the morning until eleven o'clock at night, sixteen hours of fording streams, wading through marshes, and climbing hillsides, while myriads of hungry mosquitoes bit them without ceasing. That day they covered over thirty miles, and Hearne, limping and crippled, was still with them when they reached another moss fire kindled by the women.

"They slept here last night," declared the warriors, after examining the trampled moss and the embers of a tiny fire. "Women seldom travel more than ten or twelve miles a day. We will go on walking until we overtake them."

Hearne and his companions reached the women's camp at two o'clock in the morning. While the exhausted warriors ate hungrily and then wrapped themselves in their sleeping robes, Hearne bathed his bleeding feet by the light of the campfire, washed out as much of the soil and gravel as he could, and applied medicine and bandages. So ended the hardest journey he had ever undertaken. With a sixty-pound pack on his shoulders, he had managed to keep up with lightly burdened warriors for a distance of nearly two hundred miles, across some of the world's worst country for travelers. He had left a trail of blood behind him for over a hundred miles. A weaker man, or one less determined than Hearne, would have dropped behind and died of cold or hunger. Hearne had performed an incredible feat of endurance; yet, in the journals he kept of all his travels, he never again referred to his own sufferings on the march.

Early in August, Hearne's party sighted Peshew Lake, where they had left most of their wives and all their children two months before.

Wandering parties of other Indians had increased the size of the camp to about forty tents, and the place now resembled a small Indian village. Surrounded by barking dogs and yelling children, Hearne limped into the tent Matonabi's wives erected for him.

That evening he and Matonabi ate together by the fire. The countryside was full of deer, and the deer-thong nets in the lake were bringing up great catches of fish daily. Now that the Indians were well fed and comfortable, they were in no hurry to move on southward.

"We will stay here for ten days," Matonabi told Hearne. "Our warriors are weary of traveling, and the muscles of their legs are most painful. They need time to make new moccasins for themselves to protect their injured feet. I will get my wives to cure ten fine deerskins to make you a new suit as well, for I see that your clothes are ragged and very full of holes. You will not grow weary of this delay?"

Hearne shook his head. "No, I will not grow weary. I am sorry to learn that your men have suffered so much. By all means let us rest until they have fully recovered."

"You and I are good friends," Matonabi declared solemnly. He did not notice the expression of relief and amusement on Hearne's lean, weather-darkened face.

Chapter Nine

A Lonely Camper

FOR ten days Hearne sat in his tent, thankful to be resting on soft buffalo robes and eating freshly cooked meals. Now he had time to fill pages of his journal with descriptions of the Indian way of life. He was amazingly observant, and since he was the first European to live among the Chipewyans, all that he wrote about was new to the civilized world. Indeed, he was the only European explorer who was ever able to gather such an enormous amount of information about them, for a few years later nearly all the Chipewyan tribe, and a great many of the Cree tribe, were dead of smallpox.

Food, sledges, Indian dogs, tents, bows and arrows, birch-rind kettles, and snowshoes were only a few of the subjects he mentioned. Hearne also wrote page after page of information about arctic birds and animals, which later were read eagerly by naturalists throughout Europe.

At the end of the ten days, tents were taken down, loads were strapped onto the backs of the bushy-haired dogs, sledges were laden, and Hearne's party set off on the southward trail. There were only fifty or sixty men and women now, for the rest of the Indians had taken paths of their own.

The long rest had cured Hearne's injured feet, and he had no trouble keeping up with the easy pace set by the men. Matonabi's Indians were now back in their familiar hunting grounds. Deer, partridge, and moose roamed the wild plains in great numbers, and the warriors were able to snare and shoot enough animals to supply the party with all the food and clothing they needed. But they were conscious all the while that the arctic winter was creeping along behind them, and every day they walked another nine or ten miles to the southward. A young Indian woman became sick and was left behind in the customary manner, lying beside a fire with a supply of dried meat sufficient to last her a few days. Hearne, his kindly heart bursting with pity, saw the unfortunate woman overtake his party three times. "At length, poor creature," he wrote, "she dropped behind again, and no one attempted to go back for her."

Through whirling snowstorms and showers of sleet, Matonabi's party tramped on until they reached the shores of Point Lake. There they found the first few woods, small and scrubby though they were, which they had seen since leaving the Coppermine River.

"We will camp here for a few days," said Matonabi. "This winter will be cold and long. We must make heavy clothes for the days to come, and snowshoes and sledges. Also, our women will have to prepare great supplies of dried meat, for I fear that the countryside ahead of us will be short of game."

Matonabi was right. The wind changed to the northwest and blew with unceasing fury. Thick ice formed on all the lakes and streams, and the newly built sledges ran easily over the frozen surface of freshly fallen snow.

"October came in very roughly," fur-clad Hearne wrote in his diary. "On the night of the sixth a heavy gale of wind from the Northwest put us in great confusion, for though the few woods we passed had furnished us with tent poles and fuel, our worn tents did not afford us the least shelter whatever. The wind blew with such violence that, in spite of all our efforts, it overturned several of our tents. Mine, amongst the rest, shared this disaster. The butt ends of the tent poles fell on the quadrant, and although the instrument was in a wooden box, it was broken and rendered entirely useless."

So went Hearne's second quadrant. Without it he was no longer able to determine latitudes, and his accurate map making came to an end. But he had completed the task of mapping the country through which he had passed, all the way to the Arctic Ocean and southward again to the east end of Great Slave Lake. Within a few more years, all the land south of that lake was to become familiar territory to fur traders and explorers.

On Christmas Eve in 1771, Hearne reached the northern shore of Lake Athabaska. Seven hundred miles away, across a freezing wilderness of rivers, plains, and low, ice-capped hills, lay Prince of Wales Fort and the end of his journey. The sun appeared above the horizon for only a little while during those short midwinter days. Even at its highest point it never rose above the tall pine trees which surrounded the great lake. Yet the stars and the northern lights were so brilliant that at midnight, even without any light from the moon, Hearne was able to write in his journal or read small print.

Hearne, with Matonabi and his Indians, began to cross the frozen lake. For a distance of sixty miles they made their way past little islands covered with deep snow, on which grew fine tall poplars, birches, and pines. On some of these islands they found beaver, and on all of them were big fat deer. Sometimes the Indians spent a whole day fishing in the lake with their nets. They did this by chopping holes a few feet apart from each other in the ice. Then they fastened a net to one end of a rope, and with a long stick pushed the rope from one hole to another under the ice. By the time they had pushed the rope through thirty or forty holes, the hundred-yard-long net was fully extended beneath the frozen surface. Heavy stones dangled from the bottom edge of the net to keep it upright in the slow but ceaseless currents of the water. Lake Athabaska was wonderfully rich in fish, for when the Indians hauled up their nets they found great quantities of pike, trout, perch, and barbel. Some of the fish measured from two to four feet in length, and sometimes the trout weighed thirty-five to forty pounds.

"On our arrival at the south side of Lake Athabaska, the scene was agreeably altered. Instead of the jumble of rocks and hills which composed the land on the north side, there was a fine level country, in which there was not a hill to be seen or a stone to be found."

Hearne's watch stopped just as he reached the southern side of the lake. It never worked again, and so he was unable to count the number of hours they walked every day and thus estimate the distance covered. Without a watch or a quadrant he was now no better off than the earliest explorers of America, but he kept on with the daily task of filling in his map, although much of it was guesswork. For years afterward, copies of this map were used by fur-seeking explorers.

"It would be wiser for us to walk toward the southwest for a while, instead of eastward to the fort," Matonabi told Hearne when they were encamped on the southern side of Lake Athabaska. "We need new tents and moccasins for the last stage of our journey to the shore of Hudson Bay. The weather is too cold for us to prepare such things here. Moose and buffalo skins must be soaked and then dried by the heat and smoke of a fire for several days. Afterward they must be soaked in warm water again, then dried slowly once more beside a fire. The Athabaskan Indians are very expert at making tents and clothing this way, and they always carry good supplies of skins with them. No doubt we shall be able to obtain everything we want by barter."

Hearne's last pair of moccasins were almost worn out, and his tent was a drafty ruin. He had become so accustomed to the Indians' wandering ways of travel that an extra month or two on the journey made no difference to him.

"Let us go in the direction you suggest until the end of January," he said. "That will still leave us with plenty of time to reach the fort by early summer."

Matonabi nodded approvingly. "And there will be much food on the way," he said, "for when the snow begins to melt, we can chase moose and buffalo on snowshoes. Since these animals are much heavier than men, they break through the frozen surface. A hunter can thus overtake and kill one of them in less than a day."

They swung southwestward and started trudging up the high eastern bank of the Athabaska River. The river was a couple of miles wide, and on its shore grew magnificent forests of pine, poplar, and birch. Hearne was the first explorer to see these great woods and to walk beside the Athabaska River. Not until twenty years later did another European follow this same route.

"On the eleventh of January, as some of my companions were hunting, they saw a track of a strange snowshoe. They followed it and came to a little hut, where they discovered a young woman sitting alone. . . . She proved to be one of the Western Dogrib Indians, who had been taken prisoner by the Athabaskan Indians in the summer of 1770. The following summer, when the Indians that took her prisoner were near this part, she ran away from them with the intention of returning to her own country. But the distance being so great, and having, after she was taken prisoner, been carried in a canoe the whole way, she had forgotten the direction. She built the hut in which we found her to protect herself from the winter. Here she had lived for seven months."

Hearne was amazed at the clever way in which the young woman had managed to make a comfortable little home for herself in this wild land of forest and river. She had plaited snares with the sinews taken from rabbits' legs, and kept herself supplied with partridge, squirrels, and other small game. With the skins of rabbits, and also those of a few beaver she had managed to kill, she had made a suit of neat, warm clothing for the winter. Using the inner bark of willow trees, she had plaited a 600-foot length of fine strong cord with which she had already begun to make a fishing net.

"Five or six inches of an iron hoop made into a knife, and the shank of an iron arrowhead, which served her as an awl, were the only metals this poor woman had with her when she ran away. Yet with these implements she had made herself complete snowshoes and several other useful articles. . . . Her method of making a fire was very curious, for she had no materials other than two hard flints. These, by hard knocking, produced a few sparks which at length kindled some dry touchwood. [The touchwood was made from dried fungus which the woman had collected from birch and poplar trees. It could be easily ignited by a spark.] But as this method was very troublesome and not always a success, the woman did not let her fire go out all the winter. . . . It was obvious that she was not in want of anything when we found her. There was a small stock of provisions in her hut, and she was in good health and condition. I think she was one of the finest Indian women I have seen in any part of North America."

Matonabi, who could never quite get the idea into his head that seven wives were enough for any man, even a chieftain like himself, suggested marrying this clever young woman. His other wives disapproved very loudly, and a long argument took place in their tent. Matonabi gave up his idea, and a number of the young warriors proceeded to wrestle one another that evening to see which of them would become the husband. Hearne was delighted to see that Keelshies, the Indian for whom he had an unusual dislike, was among the first losers.

The Dogrib Indian girl quietly went to live in her new husband's tent, taking with her all the clever articles she had made during her lonely stay in the wilderness. For a long time afterward, Hearne wondered whether she ever found her way back to her own people, who lived so far to the westward.

There were plenty of signs of the Athabaskan Indians, but the tribe had wandered off elsewhere for the time being. Although the snow lay deep on the ground, Matonabi's warriors came to places where moss was still smoldering from fires which had blazed there the previous autumn. They also found a broken and useless canoe, scattered bones which had been gnawed by Indian dogs, and a discarded sledge.

"They have gone south," said Matonabi. "No doubt we could overtake them if we traveled fast."

But the end of January, 1772, had come, and

Hearne was anxious to complete his journey back to the fort. "No," he replied. "Our moccasins may be worn out and our tents useless, but it is time for us to go eastward again."

They had walked nearly forty miles beside the Athabaska River. Now they swung toward the distant fort and began the last stretch of their expedition.

"As game of all kinds was very plentiful, we made only short day's journeys, and often remained two or three days in one place to eat up the results of our hunting. The woods through which we had to pass were in many places so thick that it was necessary to cut a path before the women could pass with their sledges. In other places so much of the woods had formerly been set on fire and burnt, that we were often obliged to walk farther than we otherwise should have done, before we could find green brush enough to floor our tents."

Even after spending so long a time in the company of Indians, Hearne was still unable to grow accustomed to their extraordinary selfishness and cruelty. Whereas other explorers became quickly used to the savage customs of the tribes they knew, and took little notice of them,

Hearne always grew wrathful when he witnessed an act of wickedness by the northern Indians. One day in February he wrote in his journal:

> "We saw the tracks of strangers, and some of my companions went searching for them. Finding them to be poor inoffensive people, they plundered them not only of the few furs they had, but took also one of their young women from them. Every fresh act of violence committed by my companions on the poor and distressed increased my indignation and dislike."

With ruined tents and frayed clothing, Hearne's party continued to steer eastward across a wild but beautiful region of forests, lakes, and rivers. The month of February brought violent blizzards and nights so cold that great trees burst in half from the cruel intensity of the frost. And yet the Indians continued to live well, eating beaver, deer, fish, and great steaks of buffalo and moose daily. At night they set their tents in a ring round a blazing log fire, and inside each tent there burned a smaller fire.

Long ago Hearne had abandoned his European ideas of cold and heat. When he described spending a "fairly warm and comfortable night" in his tent, he meant that the temperature was not more than ten degrees below freezing. Similarly, "bright sunshine and warm weather" indicated that it had been twenty or thirty degrees above zero during their day's march across that gleaming white countryside, crisscrossed by irregular black patches of forest.

Spring was approaching, and as Hearne traveled east, his party grew in numbers. Deerskin-clad warriors trudged along on their creaking snowshoes, and behind them came the women, hauling heavy sledges laden with bales of fur. Older children were provided with their own smaller snowshoes, and those too young to keep up with the party traveled in bark cradles on their mothers' backs. By the beginning of March there were about two hundred Indians in Hearne's party, all of them traveling toward the fort for the annual barter of furs. From some of these Indians, Matonabi managed to get a number of freshly cured skins with which to make new tents and moccasins for his party.

The spring thaw began toward the end of March, and soon Hearne was walking across a wet and windy countryside. His journal became full of the strange Indian names of the places he passed, places which no other European had ever seen. There were Wholdyeah-chuck'd-Whoie, or Large Pike Lake, and Noo-shetht-Whoie, which meant Hill Island Lake, and, finally, the Thee-lee-aza River, where Hearne first noticed swan flying northward for the summer. His parchment map was soiled and greasy and frayed by this time, but every night he continued to fill in carefully all these strange new names. Then April came, and as the snow melted, bare ground appeared in places. Geese, duck, and cranes were flying overhead in great numbers, and Hearne knew that he was nearly home.

They came at last to the upper reaches of a river which flowed into Hudson Bay. There Hearne saw his northern Indians attempt another act of cruelty.

It was Keelshies, the dark, bandy-legged little rascal, who planned the deed. He was particularly jealous of a Copper Indian who had decided to accompany Hearne's party southward to sell a magnificent bale of furs. When the

Indians began to cross the river in their canoes, Keelshies contrived the loading arrangements so that this Copper Indian was left behind until the last. The bale of furs belonging to him, his bow and arrows, and a leather bag containing his clothing were brought across the river in the first canoes to cross. Keelshies then motioned to his wives to load the poor man's baggage onto their own sledges, and casually joined the rest of the party as it prepared to continue the march. The Copper Indian was left standing alone on the northern bank of the river, deprived of everything he owned. The river was too dangerous to swim, for it was wide, deep, and choked with ice. In other words, Keelshies was deliberately leaving the wretched man to die of hunger in a foreign countryside.

The crowd of Indians glanced casually at the distant figure, then picked up their bundles or adjusted the yoke lines of the sledges round their chests and foreheads. They were so accustomed to cruelty and death that this incident meant nothing to them. The man was a Copper Indian, and a stranger to the group. If Keelshies was clever enough to obtain the man's furs, that was entirely his own affair. Even Matonabi, who was more humane than the rest of the Chipewyan tribe, began leaving the riverbank.

"Just a moment," said Hearne. "That man yonder. We can't leave him there."

Matonabi shrugged his wide leather-clad shoulders. "It was Keelshies who wanted the man's furs. There is nothing we can do."

"Oh, yes there is," said Hearne, now thoroughly enraged. "We can go back and get him."

"Keelshies will be angry," said Matonabi. "He will lose the furs he has taken."

"If you don't go back," said Hearne, "I will."

Matonabi stared at him curiously for a moment. "Keelshies has done this before," he said. "He once left twelve Copper Indians on an island in the middle of a lake. They had sold their furs at the fort and were returning to their own country with good axes and muskets and blankets. All twelve of them died of hunger on the island. I will show you the island in another two days' journey."

"Are you going back to get that man," asked Hearne, "or am I?"

Matonabi, grumbling under his breath, his dark face sulky, took a canoe from another Indian, launched it, and set off across the river. He returned in a little while, bringing the Copper Indian with him. Hearne escorted the rescued man into Keelshies' presence and stood by while the Indian picked up his belongings and the precious bale of furs. Keelshies did nothing. The expression on Hearne's face warned him that silence was wise, and the Indian knew that this white man was now as tough and experienced as himself.

Spring had come by this time, and the forests were changing to a lighter, brighter green. Great flocks of birds were migrating northward daily, and a few early flowers were appearing in the deposits of soil among the rocks. But even at this time Hearne and his Indians suffered fresh miseries from the bad weather.

"On the night of May 1, a heavy fall of snow came on, which was followed by a hard gale of wind. At that time we were on the top of a high barren hill, a considerable distance from any woods. Judging it to be no more than a squall, we sat down in expectation of its soon passing by. As the night advanced, however, the gale increased so much that

it was impossible for a man to stand upright. We were obliged to lie down without any other defence against the weather than putting our sledges to windward of us. These were of no real service, as they only harbored a great drift of snow, which in some places covered us to a depth of two or three feet."

And yet, only ten days later, on May 11, 1772, they threw away their snowshoes, which had become useless on the bare ground exposed by the melting snow.

"Good weather all the way to the fort now," said Matonabi. "Soon you will be with your friends again."

Matonabi was wrong. Bad weather hit them again on May 19, and Hearne wrote that his party was "often obliged to wade above the knees through swamps of mud, water, and wet snow."

Over the Dubawnt River they went, then across the ice on Snowbird Lake, and so to Cath-a-wha-chaga River, which they navigated in a howling rainstorm. On May 28, Hearne saw the ugly gray waters of the Seal River, its surface covered with broken ice and blackened tree trunks, flowing swiftly toward Hudson Bay. He knew then that he was within fifty miles of Prince of Wales Fort.

On May 29, Samuel Hearne made his last entry in the battered and mud-stained journal which had traveled so long and so far in his shoulder pack.

> "I arrived in good health at Prince of Wales Fort. Though my discoveries are not likely to prove of any great advantage to the Nation, I have the pleasure to think that I have carried out my orders and put a final end to all disputes concerning a Northwest Passage through Hudson Bay."

In return for all his hardships, sufferings, and risks, Hearne received as a reward from the grateful Hudson's Bay Company the small sum of 200 pounds ($600). The Company recovered most of this money by selling copies of his beautiful map. But at least Hearne achieved fame as the first man to reach the arctic by the overland route.

Chapter Ten

The Fort Builder

GOVERNOR MOSES NORTON died at the
end of December, 1773, about eighteen months
after Hearne got back to the fort. The Governor's manners and habits had not improved
during his last couple of years, and his
jealousy of Hearne had become much greater.

Norton died most ungraciously. His last remark, addressed to one of his Indian wives, who was standing near his bedside, was, "Confound you for an idle creature! If I live I'll knock out your brains."

There were changes at Prince of Wales Fort after Norton's death. The directors of the Hudson's Bay Company had been growing increasingly alarmed at the new competition they were meeting in the fur trade. Their practice had been to build forts, fill them with European traders and clerks, and wait for the Indians to bring furs for sale from hundreds, and sometimes thousands, of miles away. But down in Montreal a group of Scottish-Canadian merchants had different ideas about running the fur trade. They formed the Northwest Company and started sending their own traders into the heart of Indian country to barter for furs.

Some of these men were French-Canadian *voyageurs*. They were experts with a canoe, accustomed to the prairies and forests, and often able to speak many different Indian dialects. Others were American frontiersmen who had served their apprenticeship in the fur trade in the valley of the Mississippi. Many of them were Scottish Highlanders, the sons of the soldiers who had fought under General Wolfe to win Canada from the French. All these men, though undisciplined, were self-reliant and courageous. They spent most of their lives traveling enormous distances in birch-bark canoes, down howling river rapids and across storm-swept lakes. Some of them drowned or froze to death. Others were killed by the Indians or by a drunken European companion. But these men knew how to trade with the tribes, and they brought back enormous quantities of furs to the warehouses of the Northwest Company in Montreal.

The men of the Hudson's Bay Company contemptuously called these Canadian rivals the Master Pedlars. But the directors in London were worried. Their own trade was falling off, and their profits were going down. Unless they did something quickly, the Northwest Company would seize the entire fur trade.

Up to the present we've built all our forts along the shores of Hudson Bay, thought the directors. Now we'll have to start building other trading posts in Indian country, where the tribes will only have to travel short distances to bring us their furs for sale.

They wrote to young Matthew Cocking, the second in command at York Factory on the west coast of Hudson Bay, and asked him to make an overland journey inland to find a good site for this proposed new trading post.

Cocking was a good traveler, and he was lucky that the route lay across prairies inhabited by Indians far superior to those whom Hearne had met on his northern journey. These tribes had good horses, well-made clothing, and cleaner habits. They cultivated their own tobacco and cooked in earthen pots. Cocking spent the winter of 1772 on the plains between the north and south branches of the Saskatchewan River. In the spring of 1773 he returned to York and sent his report to London.

"We'll build a factory on the Saskatchewan River," the directors decided. "One of our men already in Canada will have to take charge of the work."

"Samuel Hearne's the man," suggested an official named Andrew Graham, who had served long years in Canada and was a great admirer of Hearne's. "Put him in charge of the job and send Matthew Cocking as his assistant."

On June 23, 1774, Hearne and Cocking set out from York Factory. With them in their heavily laden canoes went Robert Longmoor, an English carpenter, and eight English workmen. These newcomers eyed with amazement and alarm the first great forests and prairies they had ever seen. They were strangers to the wilds, and they were gloomy at the prospect of setting off on a journey of 600 miles into the heart of Indian country. Hearne, however, was delighted. In these southern regions the winters were reasonably mild compared with those of the arctic. There was unlimited game, and the Indian tribes welcomed the idea of having a trading post in their own country. Life was much easier down here than in the Barren Lands, which Hearne had traversed only two years earlier.

A crooked chain of rivers and lakes ran southwest from Hudson Bay to join the great Saskatchewan River. Young Cocking was the guide now, for he had been along this route before. But it was Hearne who led the expedition.

Gradually he taught the inexperienced Englishmen how to make themselves comfortable in a tent, how to hunt game and catch fish, and how to protect themselves with bear's grease against the swarms of mosquitoes and black flies.

There were plenty of signs that the men of the Northwest Company had passed along this same route in their quest for furs. On August 5, Hearne wrote in his diary:

> "This day we passed by one of the Pedlars' houses. Although nobody is in it, it is where Lewis Primeau and seventeen others wintered last year. By the Indians' account, as soon as the ice permitted, this spring, they embarked with all their [trading] goods and proceeded to intercept the Athabaskan Indians on their way to Prince of Wales Fort."

This was the first time Hearne had seen the results of the Northwest Company's poaching in the Hudson's Bay Company's territories. There were few furs left in the Indian villages along the Saskatchewan River; the Pedlars had bought them all during the early spring of that year.

Cocking had decided that a place named Pasquia, on the Saskatchewan River, was the best site for the new trading post. Pasquia, known today as The Pas, had been the meeting place of Indian tribes for hundreds of years.

Hearne looked at it with his experienced eyes. "No," he said. "There's too much marshland round here, and marshes breed mosquitoes. Besides, there's no timber for building the trading post."

He found the ideal site after a few days of paddling up and down the river and traveling cross-country on foot. It was a level sweep of meadow beside Lake Cumberland, ringed round with heavy pine forests. By that time late August had arrived, and the surface of the lake was being swept by frequent gales.

"Cold weather's coming," said Hearne. "We'll have to build our winter quarters."

The workmen began sawing timber and digging foundations on a Monday morning. They were scared of the cold night winds, of the loneliness and silence of the surrounding forest, and of the grim befeathered Indians who came to squat on their heels and watch the work. The men felt that the sooner they were living inside good strong walls and close to a fire, the safer they would be from the dangers of this country. On Thursday they were living inside their new house, and sealing gaps between the logs with tightly packed moss. Longmoor, the carpenter, was busy with the construction of a solid log floor.

During those first few days Indian hunters brought great loads of freshly killed game to Cumberland House. "Give us brandy in exchange," they said. "The men of the Northwest Company give us all the brandy we want."

Hearne knew that they spoke the truth. The selfish Scottish directors of the Northwest Company were exchanging enormous quantities of brandy for Indian furs. As long as these directors made vast fortunes for themselves quickly, they cared not at all if the Indian hunters and trappers became drunken and useless within a few years. In other words, the Northwest Company was quickly ruining the whole future of the fur trade and the men on whom it depended. The Hudson's Bay Company, on the other hand, had started to keep spirits of any kind away from the Indians, knowing that brandy caused them to behave like wild creatures.

"I'll give you guns or blankets or brass kettles instead," Hearne replied. "We have no brandy to spare."

The Indian hunters came no more. Instead, there arrived a party of Pedlars with endless supplies of rum. They were rough but good-hearted fellows, only doing what they had been told by their directors in Montreal. Hearne was friendly toward them, but he watched disapprovingly as these rival traders proceeded to collect enormous quantities of furs in exchange for their rum. When the Pedlars left, Hearne wrote:

> "The Indian chief who came with us from the Fort and has been with us ever since, was so affected by the smell of the Canadians' New England rum that he and his crew embarked and followed after them before they [the Pedlars] were out of sight."

Now there were no Indians left at Cumberland House, and Hearne had depended on them to bring in food supplies.

"We'll die of starvation in this forsaken country when the winter clamps down hard," muttered the English workmen. "We're getting short of supplies already."

Hearne and Cocking glanced at one another and smiled. They knew how to live well in a country where the inexperienced novice would starve.

Cumberland Lake froze over until its surface was covered with a foot of ice. Hearne chopped holes and set long nets, as he had seen the northern Indians do. He made snares and brought in partridge. Cocking and he raided beaver houses in the lake, after hammering on the ice with wooden poles to make the beaver retreat to their houses. Longmoor, the carpenter, watched and began to imitate Hearne. He learned to get downwind of a grazing moose, and to enter a wood against the breeze so that wild game and birds could not hear the noise of his approach. In spite of the continuing supplies of food, the rest of the workmen remained scared and doubtful. They were convinced that such good fortune could not last.

"This scanty way of living," wrote Hearne, "being so different from the certain good allowance at the Factory, is very alarming to my men. It is with the greatest difficulty I can persuade them from thinking that entire famine must arise."

Hearne's great store of knowledge of Indian ways once saved Longmoor's legs, and perhaps his life. One day the carpenter went out to bring back a moose he had shot the evening before. He returned with both feet badly frozen. Hearne mentioned the incident in his diary.

"I remembered the remedy which I had seen Matonabi's wives use during my journey to the North. I boiled the inner rind of the larch root and used it as a dressing."

Longmoor was crippled for almost three months, but at the end of that time he was able to go back to work on the construction of the new trading post.

Winter ended early in this southern climate. Hearne was astonished to see great showers of melting snow falling from the pine trees in April and ice cracking in the spring breeze that rippled the lake. The men gazed at these signs of warmer weather and grinned at the sight of grazing deer and great flights of birds. They picked up their hammers and saws in a more cheerful state of mind. Seeing their better humor, Hearne drove them hard, from six in the morning until six at night, six days a week.

The work at Cumberland House was finished in May, 1775. Down the long waterways back to Fort York went Hearne and five of his men. The rest of the men, under Matthew Cocking, stayed behind to guard the trading post until others could be sent up to take charge.

That summer, Hearne went back to England on leave. He had spent ten years in Canada and risen to fame throughout Europe as an explorer. He was now only thirty years old.

Chapter Eleven

Prisoner of War

WHILE he was in England, Samuel Hearne went to see the directors of the Hudson's Bay Company. "Mr. Hearne," they said, "since Mr. Norton's death we have not succeeded in finding a capable man to take his place at Prince of Wales Fort. We have decided, therefore, to select you as the new governor. Do what you can to increase the whale fishery in the Bay.

And see if you can find another officer who would be willing to follow your example of exploration."

War had begun between the American colonies and England. There had been skirmishing between British regular troops at Concord and Lexington in the state of Massachusetts. This had been followed by a regular battle at Bunker Hill, which both the Americans and the English declared they had won. But the war made no difference to Hearne. He went back to the great fort on the bleak western shore of the Bay in January, 1776.

Once again Hearne was among the northern Indians, and they, in their uncouth and savage way, seemed glad to see him. Matonabi was among his first visitors.

"You are our friend," the chieftain said. "We have shared many marches and campfires together. The men of the Northwest Company are already trying to buy our furs, but we have refused to sell any to them. We northern Indians will continue to come to this fort, for we know that you will treat us well."

Matonabi spoke pleasantly, but Hearne did

not take the polite speech too seriously. He had lived a long time among these northern Indians and was not easily flattered by their words, as a less experienced European might have been. He was, in fact, already writing a warning on the subject of Indian craftiness in a manuscript he was preparing in his spare time.

"Whenever any really distressed natives come to the Company's Factory, they are always assisted with food, clothes, medicines, and every other necessity, without cost to themselves. These Indians, in return, instruct their countrymen how to behave in order to obtain the same charity. Thus it is very common to see both men and women come to the Fort half-naked, when either the severe cold in winter or the extreme troublesomeness of the flies in summer make it necessary for every part [of the body] to be covered. On those occasions they are seldom at a loss for a plausible story . . . and never fail to color this story with plenty of sighs, groans, and tears. Sometimes they pretend to be lame and even blind in order to excite pity.

"The Indians take care always to seem fond of a new Governor. They flatter his pride by telling him that they look up to him as the father of their tribe, and never fail to speak badly about the lack of generosity shown by the last Governor. If this does not have the effect they wish for, these Indians tell him to his face that he is one of the most cruel of men, that he has no feeling for the distress of their tribe, and that many have died for want of proper assistance. . . . In time, however, this kind of talk also ceases. The Indians become perfectly used to the man whom they would willingly have made a fool, and say, 'He is no child, and not to be deceived by us.'"

Queer people and queer customs! An ugly and drafty stone fort in a lonely and unattractive country! And yet Hearne settled down quite comfortably to his new work as governor. He remained friendly with Matonabi, even when that rascally fellow tried to obtain enormous presents from him every year. In October of 1776, Hearne wrote in his growing manuscript:

"My old guide, Matonabi, came at the head of a large gang of northern Indians to trade at Prince of Wales Fort. . . . I dressed him out and also clothed his six wives from top to toe. Afterwards, during his ten-day stay at the fort, he begged:

    7 uniform coats
  15 plain coats
  18 hats
  18 shirts
    8 muskets
140 pounds gunpowder

Also a great quantity of hatchets, ice chisels, files, bayonets, knives, tobacco, cloth, blankets, combs, looking glasses, stockings, and handkerchiefs."

Matonabi's demands seemed very unfair to Hearne, and he said so.

"Please yourself," said the chieftain, "but I did not expect you to make difficulties over such a small matter as this. I think that from now on, I and my countrymen will take our furs to the place where we can get our own price for them."

"Where is that?" asked Hearne, who already knew the answer.

"To the Canadian fur traders from Montreal," Matonabi replied.

Hearne handed over the presents, which were in addition to all the trade goods the Indians had already obtained for their furs. He had to keep the northern Indians coming to the fort, even if the Company was making very little profit on the deal. But so much for Matonabi's polite speech of only a few months earlier!

Two years later, Matonabi turned up at the fort with a more unusual, though much less expensive, demand. "I have always known," he said to Hearne, "that you are a clever man at witchcraft. Now this past summer, a certain man has treated me very badly, and I think he wishes to murder me. Therefore, I want you to kill him with your magic."

Hearne had known for years that Matonabi believed he was a clever witch doctor. He tried to look very solemn as he asked, "Where is this enemy of yours?"

"Quite close," Matonabi said eagerly. "Indeed, he is not more than a few hundred miles away."

"That's excellent news," Hearne replied. "I'll see what I can do."

He sat down and drew a little sketch of two human figures wrestling with one another. One of them was holding a knife pointed at the other man's breast. Close beside these two men, Hearne drew a pine tree with a human eye hovering in the air above it and a hand protruding from the trunk of the tree.

"This is you fighting with your enemy," said Hearne, pointing to the man holding the knife. "Here is my spirit, watching and helping you from the tree."

Matonabi was delighted and went back to the

great plains for the spring and summer, taking the sketch with him. That fall he returned to the fort in a happy mood, and his demands for expensive presents were much fewer than usual. "Truly you are a great and clever wizard," he told Hearne. "My enemy died this summer, and now all my troubles are ended."

For years afterward, the northern Indians were always a little afraid of Hearne, yet they came regularly to the fort and sold none of their furs to the Pedlars.

News came slowly to Hearne that France had joined the Americans in the Revolutionary War. The news did not affect life at the fort, for Hudson Bay was tucked away in the far North, and no enemy was expected there.

The French came sailing into the Bay one warm, sunny morning in July, 1782. Three men-of-war made straight for the mouth of the Churchill River and dropped anchor. Three hundred and fifty well-armed French infantrymen came ashore and prepared to attack the fort.

Hearne looked at his own garrison. There were thirty-nine clerks, traders, carpenters, and mechanics. Some of them had never fired a musket in their lives. None of them except Hearne knew how to load, train, and fire the forty-two cannons on the walls of the fort. The French troops were landing guns to spray every rampart and loophole with deadly grapeshot, and the Englishmen were already white-faced and scared.

Hearne surrendered. There was nothing else he could do, for that great cumbersome fort needed at least two hundred trained men to hold its walls against an attacking enemy.

The clerks and bookkeepers were taken aboard the French vessels. Hearne himself became a prisoner on the flagship, where he met Admiral La Pérouse, who was soon to become one of France's greatest explorers. The two men became good friends from their first meeting. La Pérouse was forty-one years old; Hearne was thirty-seven. La Pérouse dreamed of exploring the still unknown coasts of far-off oceans; Hearne had already explored north of the Arctic Circle.

"If you will permit," said La Pérouse, "I would like to read this journal of your voyage northward to the Coppermine River. And as a geographer of some small reputation in France, I would be honored by your permission to study the maps you have made."

They spent long evenings together in the Admiral's fine oak-paneled stateroom in the stern of the flagship. Eagerly La Pérouse examined Hearne's fine charts and read page after page describing the journey by land to the far North.

"This is a magnificent story," said La Pérouse. "Promise me, my friend, that when you are released—and as a civilian you will not remain long a prisoner—you will publish your book in England. You have written so much that is new to the entire world."

"If you think it worth publishing, sir," replied Hearne, "I will gladly give you my promise."

One of the Company's ships entered the Bay and was promptly seized by the French. "Go back to England in this vessel," La Pérouse told Hearne. "Take your men with you. We, too, are leaving the Bay, and I fear that our seizure of your foodstuffs would cause hunger among you were you to remain here during the coming winter."

The ships sailed away, and the desolate shores of the Bay became silent, except for the constant crying of the sea birds. When Matonabi and his Chipewyan Indians arrived at the fort that fall, they found it empty. The great walls were broken in places where the French had vainly tried to destroy them with charges of gunpowder.

A few wandering Indians told Matonabi what had happened. "An enemy came with great ships and many men. They took away your friend and all those who were with him at the fort. We do not know where they have gone, or if they are still alive."

Matonabi became silent, and his heart was filled with a great despair. Even though he was a northern Indian he had a feeling of true friendship for Hearne. It distressed him greatly to think that his former comrade might be dead.

A few weeks later, Matonabi slipped quietly out of his camp one night and hanged himself from the branch of a pine tree.

Hearne came back the next year, long after poor Matonabi was dead and his grieving tribe had returned to the northland. Prince of Wales

Fort was never rebuilt, for the Company had realized that the place was too big and cumbersome. Hearne was given the job of building a new and smaller fort five miles up the Churchill River. Meanwhile, Hearne had kept his promise to La Pérouse. His book was already in the hands of printers in London, and in 1784 it was published.

During the next few years Hearne began to realize that his long marches across the frozen arctic had injured his health. He had endured the hardships of hunger and exposure to freezing temperatures too long. Perhaps, too, he felt very deeply the loss of his old friend Matonabi. In 1787, he left Hudson Bay forever and went back to England. There he made many new friends among the people who had read his book, and argued with a few enemies. The latter were men who had tried, somewhat vainly, to go exploring on their own account in northern Canada. They had used their imaginations to fill in the gaps in their stories, and some of them had composed the most fabulous lies and written the most inaccurate information. Hearne was a truthful person who had the habit of plain speaking, and in very blunt language he corrected their lies and pointed out the errors in the books they had written.

Hearne returned to Somerset, where the warm sunshine and cool green countryside reminded him of his boyhood. Once again he followed half-remembered woodland paths and walked beside little streams where years before he had fished for trout and perch. When winter came, he scarcely noticed it. On those rare days when it was freezing, shivering country people marveled to see this big man walking without hat or coat along the chilly lanes.

"Cold?" he said, when they spoke about the bitter weather. "Why, my friends, I have known so much cold that I doubt if I will ever be properly warm again. In the land where I spent years of my life, a day like this would cause us to complain of the heat."

Hearne did not live long enough to see his fast-selling book published in a French edition. He died in 1792, and the book did not appear until 1795. Nor had Admiral La Pérouse lived long enough to see the event either. He had disappeared with his ship and seamen in the

year 1788, while on a voyage of exploration to the little-known island of the New Hebrides in the Pacific Ocean.

The broken walls of Prince of Wales Fort still exist today. It is possible to stand on their ramparts and look out toward the lands that were an unknown wilderness until Samuel Hearne risked his life to explore and map them.

RONALD SYME spent his boyhood sailing off the New Zealand coast or hunting wild boar in the North Island bush country. On leaving school at the age of sixteen, he went to sea in a Pacific cargo steamer and spent four years trading between Australia, New Zealand, San Francisco, and the South Sea Islands. At eighteen, while still at sea, he began writing short stories. In 1934 Mr. Syme left the sea to become a professional writer. Between then and the outbreak of war, he lived in Algiers, Alexandria, Vienna, Rome, Trieste, and Paris.

In 1939 he joined the British Merchant Service as a gunner and saw action in the North Atlantic until the end of 1940. Because he could speak four languages, he was then transferred to the British Army Intelligence Corps. After fighting with the Eighth Army in Africa, he became a paratrooper during the Italian campaign.

After the war he settled down to writing again. He is now a well-known author in the United States, and in England, where he is also recognized as a distinguished scholar. An insatiable voyager, he still continues to visit various portions of the globe, for research or pleasure. He recently sailed 1660 miles in a twenty-ton schooner from New Zealand to Rarotonga in the Cook Islands.